'I gobble[...] [...] mother, or otherwise – to do the same' Pandora Sykes

'Remarkable' Lorraine Kelly

'I absolutely loved *I Am Not Your Baby Mother*' Giovanna Fletcher

'Brilliant' Sophie Ellis-Bextor

'An essential exploration of the realities of Black motherhood in the UK' *Observer*

'Every mother, everywhere, should read this book' *OK!*

'The woman bringing a fresh perspective to the mumfluencer world' *Grazia*

'A game-chang[...] [...] *Red*

'A brilliantly o[...] [...]other' *Closer*

'[An] original [...] [...]vigating Black motherhood' *Cosmopolitan*

'Written in her brilliantly witty manner, this book is every Black British woman's motherhood manual' Refinery 29

'She's the straight-talking social-media star who hates the word "influencer", refuses to "dress small" and is on a mission to portray a vision of motherhood inclusive of race and class' *Stella*

'An observant and timely guide' *Evening Standard*

'Important and necessary' *i*

'Packed with insight for all women, whatever your race or parental status' *Women's Health*

'The must-read book of the summer' *Mother and Baby*

'Brilliant [...] as much an astoundingly good read as it is an essential one' *Good Housekeeping*

Candice Brathwaite is the hugely popular influencer, writer and founder of Make Motherhood Diverse – an online initiative that aims to encourage a more accurately representative and diverse depiction of motherhood in the media. She has appeared on countless panels to discuss modern motherhood. Her writing has appeared in *Stylist*, the *Metro* and the *Huffington Post*. *I Am Not Your Baby Mother* is her first book. She lives in Milton Keynes with her husband and two children.

I AM NOT YOUR BABY MOTHER

What it's like to be a black British mother

Candice Brathwaite

Quercus

First published in hardback in Great Britain in 2020 by
Quercus Editions Ltd

This paperback published in 2021 by

Quercus Editions Ltd
Carmelite House
50 Victoria Embankment
London EC4Y 0DZ

An Hachette UK company

A CIP catalogue record for this book is available
from the British Library

ISBN 978 1 52940 628 3
Ebook ISBN 978 1 52940 626 9

10 9 8 7 6 5 4 3 2 1

Typeset by CC Book Production
Printed and bound in Great Britain by Clays Ltd, Elcograf S.p.A.

Papers used by Quercus are from well-managed forests and other responsible sources.

For Esmé-Olivia and Richard Junior.

This book was published during a universally testing time.

It is almost as if the entire world is on fire.

*Although it will perhaps never again be of this magnitude,
there will be many more fires throughout both of your lives.*

*Always remember that you possess enough water
to fight those flames.*

All my love,

Mummy

CONTENTS

INTRODUCTION

The bedazzled characters which gyrated across the screen of my own mother's TV were decorated in ensembles which mimicked the ones I had spotted on the VHS cover of the salacious movie *Dancehall Queen*. I say spotted on the cover, because with its hypersexual references and bad language, I wasn't allowed to watch *Dancehall Queen* until many years later – but from the picture on the cover alone, I knew what to liken these characters to – the only difference being that these young black British women weren't trying to secure themselves as head monarch of any bacchanal or ballroom; instead they were trying to navigate life whilst being regarded as what is often painted as one of the lowliest in black British society: a baby mother.

Now to be clear, as I would never want anyone to say that I'm lackadaisical in my understanding, the Oxford English Dictionary explanation of the meaning of the word baby-mother is as follows:

babymother; noun: the mother of one or more of
a man's children, who is not his wife or current
partner.

Origin: 1960s: from **baby** + **mother**, after **babyfather**;
originally in Caribbean English.

Before the term 'babymother' was co-opted by the main-stream and repackaged as this cool title often edited to the Americanised 'Baby Mama', within the thickened walls of the black community it was quite literally the mark of the beast.

'Now don't you become someone's baby mother!' my father would warn. 'You're better than that!'

'Try and get married first,' aunties would advise. 'It just sets a better *tone*.'

'All I know is, I don't want to be with no baby mother,' I'd overhear less than suitable bachelors, already four kids deep, chant whilst I sat in the barbershop.

To have a child out of wedlock seemed to be quite a new cultural shift within black society, especially since the society of which I speak was only just being acknowledged by the British. My own nan and grandad hastily threw themselves up the aisle once they both clocked that my nan's period hadn't been left on the shore of a beach in Barbados, but instead had been halted due to the physical storytelling of their young love and her womb was now heavy with the perceived burden of sin, which they quickly had to rectify in order to not be 'shamed'.

This feeling was perhaps compounded by having to navigate the move to the UK not even a decade after the Windrush. Continuing learned protocol, they both knew that in order to celebrate what would go on to be my mother's life, they had to be seen to be committed both in the eyes of the church and more relevantly, their very nosy community.

But in the late 80s and early 90s, a new trend began to emerge. Be it based on self-prophesised propaganda or the complicated effects stemming from layered issues related to race and gender which deserve to be scrutinised in another book, what seemed to be happening is that some young black women were being left holding a baby and not much else. And for those who had pondered on doing the leaving because they had perhaps been stuck in a relationship more ill-fitting than an Instagram shop outfit, they now felt as though feminism had extended its white hand towards them and they could finally decide to raise a child alone, without the heat of shame warming their neck.

But no matter how these women ended up alone was besides the point. Society had made up its mind that black mothers would find their layers of womanhood, and the other details and nuances which made them individuals, stripped away, and they were relegated to being mere baby mothers. The entire embodiment of their personal self seemed to be cast aside because they made the most selfless decision of all, which was to raise their child regardless of their current relationship status.

'I am not your baby mother, I am the mother of your child!' I remember hearing a faceless woman spit at an equally faceless man one day.

And now the term 'baby mother' isn't just a succession of piercing words solely cast upon single black mothers, it's become a label which is used primarily to dismantle and disable the legitimacy of black women's version of motherhood in general. It's used in a way to demean and perhaps unintentionally put a red mark through any ideas along the lines of assimilating black motherhood with positivity and success.

And for that reason alone, the fear of becoming a baby mother, I perhaps resisted the idea of having my own children. There are far more layers to my nonchalance towards becoming a mother, which we will unravel within the pages of this book, but as with most appropriated things, it seems that only the ones who feel strangulated by the negative stereotype at hand seem to want to do away with the respective term altogether.

I personally don't want to reclaim the term baby mother. It can stay on the shelf, thanks. I want black women, black women who happen to be mothers, to be given space to share their multifaceted motherhood journeys – irrespective of their family make-up, current financial situation or number of past lovers – with pride. I want black women to know that their version of motherhood is as righteous and as sacred as any other and deserves to be as protected as any other woman's. I want black mothers to be able to share their worries about pregnancy, their birth stories (be they traumatic, tragic or testimonial) and beyond, because that's what their white female counterparts have been doing for decades and, I must add, getting paid very well for.

When we think about black British women being depicted as mothers in the media, what's the first thing that comes to mind, if anything at all? Is it a well-to-do-looking woman, sitting cross-legged in a vegan cafe breastfeeding her baby whilst reading a book about transcendental meditation? Or is it a loud-mouthed caricature who doesn't seem to be enjoying motherhood at all?

I've desperately craved a space where I can discuss my motherhood journey, openly and honestly, all whilst capturing the original moments which make being a black British mother so unique. I want the space to talk about the fact that black women in the UK are five times more likely to die in childbirth than their white counterparts. I desire the space to talk about how when I thought about naming my children I was purposeful in my decision to be mindful of names which could perhaps be defined as '*ghetto*'. I deserve the space to speak about how the minute I found out I was pregnant with my son, that my partner and I felt that this was our sign to get out of London, for fear of having to prematurely bury him due to the spike in knife crime which primarily sees black boys at both ends of the blade.

This book will be part memoir and part manifesto, a

tell-all and self-help book combined. Quite frankly, it's the
book I wish I was gifted when I found out I was pregnant.
Primarily, I hope this book helps black British mothers feel
validated and encouraged to take up space. For all others
reading it, I hope I'm able to help accurately describe the
many hurdles black British mothers are up against. And I
want to add that even if you aren't a black mother, that doesn't
mean that this book isn't for you. In more ways than one,
it will perhaps be better for you than anyone else, because
dismantling this unfair and incorrect negative stereotype is
going to take group effort.

And finally I want all to know that:

I may have a baby.

I may be a mother.

But I am not your baby mother.

1

THE BLUEST LINE

To set the tone of this book, I need to begin with disarming honesty. That's the way I like to live my life, you see. I think it is the best way to protect yourself; to dig deep down into that proverbial basket of 'dirty laundry' and proudly hang it out in the street for all to see.

So, here goes: I never wanted children.

So much so, that when my contraception failed me in my early twenties, I knew without a shadow of a doubt that an abortion was the way to go.

Now, I want to start by telling you this for two reasons. Firstly, within the black community, something as personal and 'unclean' as an abortion is supposed to be kept secret. Continuing the theme of having to play up and into a role of perceived public perfection, I have known many black women who have carried the weight of their swollen belly and its abrupt but necessary ending in silence, because we come from a place where you aren't supposed to subject yourself and your foetus to such a thing.

Secondly, I want to develop a relationship with you, the reader, that is rooted in trust. I've built a career on being as authentic as possible, no matter how overused that term now is, and I think it would be grossly unfair of me to paint an insincere picture of myself.

Now, I'm fully aware that my revelation might have already made you fling this book across the room with anger. Maybe you're like the many pockets of states in the USA who, often for religious reasons, feel that a woman should bring forth life no matter her circumstances. Maybe you're a man who feels entitled to a woman's body, to determine her choices. Whatever the case, I am pro-choice, and back then my abortion was the right choice for me – especially as I was newly single and in my early twenties.

Raising a child on my own was never something I longed to do, primarily because of what I saw friends of a similar age experience and being the eldest of three to a single mother. As far as I'd seen, the job of being someone's mother was usually rooted in hardship and very rarely celebrated. At family functions, mothers sat in circles, similar to those found in church, bemoaning their chores, responsibilities and the fact that they felt like they'd given up bright futures for the young children who sat at their feet in forced silence, because their babies were being raised to be 'seen and not heard'.

Coupled with the fact that my instinct warned me that

the man I had fallen pregnant to was not going to be winning any Father of the Year awards, I knew deep down that not bringing a child into an already precarious situation was what was right for me.

Five years after that abortion, I was faced with another blue line illustrating that I was still as fertile as my ancestors, and I felt exactly the same as I did the first time. Although this time I wasn't single and I knew the child would be born into an abundance of love, I still felt incapable of being a mother.

I had to ask myself, why. I was no longer in my early twenties, so I didn't have to fear being socially chastised for being 'too young'. In fact, many female family members had recently taken to asking me if everything was OK 'down there' because at twenty-six, there was an expectation for me to have long since thrown myself at the pearly gates of motherhood, even if the resounding belief was that it was more hell than heaven. I was in love with my partner and although we weren't as financially secure as I would have liked, if I was honest with myself, that wasn't the reason I didn't feel ready or able to have a child.

I needed to look beyond my present circumstances and instead look back to when I was a baby to begin to understand my complex relationship with motherhood. My upbringing was unique because I was raised primarily by my maternal grandfather. Shortly before I was born, he was mugged. It was a violent crime that left him blind in one eye and no longer able to work. So when I was finally earthside and my mother wanted to return to work after having me, it was my grandad, George (or Bentley, depending on the setting in which you met him), who looked after me whilst my nan, Vonore (or Vern, as we called her), continued to head out to full-time work.

Before my father and mother had even made it up the aisle my mother found out he was cheating on her – when she was pregnant, no less. I would guess that a mixture of fear and hormones made her try to see past his philandering, but a mere eight months after I was born, my mother made the difficult choice to split up with him and raise me as a single parent. And although I can truthfully attest that I never, ever heard my father refer to her as such, in the eyes of a judgemental society, my mother became a 'baby mother'.

After having me, she remained living at home with my grandparents, giving her immediate access to a support unit which many parents now pay a few thousand for per month. I've been told that since I was tiny, my uncle, who was a year my mother's junior, was at my side. My nan made sure to have my passport ready by the time I was five months because she had already booked a holiday to Barbados where she planned to show me off to all her brothers and sisters.

But neither my mum, my uncle, my nan or her brothers and sisters were available to look after me, and so the role fell to my grandad, the jewel in our family crown, the most constant and consistent man in my life. A short, caramel-skinned man with a sharp wit, a wide smile peppered with flecks of gold and a wealth of wisdom. When my mother declared that she wanted to return to work, he didn't hesitate to encourage her to leave me at home with him. I think it secretly gave him purpose. He had fallen into a deep depression since having to give up work and being able to take up the role of my primary carer gave him something to focus on. He may have lost the sight in one eye, but the good one was always fixed upon me. So whilst my mother and my nan, the women of the household, went out to acquire the bacon, it was just us.

From as far back as I can remember, I knew nothing but his strict and loving ways. He gave me all the physical comfort I needed and carried out his matriarchal duties with unconditional skill and dedication. He believed that a routine was the best way to establish intellectual brilliance and he never swayed from this from morning till night – unless we were watching the WWE's *Royal Rumble* or, years later, the OJ Simpson trial, when bedtime came around, both of which in his own Bentley way, he deemed as educational.

He would wake me up at 7am and instruct me to brush my teeth, after which he would use a warm, wet flannel to dampen my face and remove the crusted sleep out of the corner of my eyes. If it was summer, he would run me the shallowest of bucket baths – though it wasn't actually a bucket but more of a basin – which was just about wide enough for me to kneel in. As I grew up, I chuckled at the memory of this, mainly because the basin was within a bath. What was the point of that? I guess there are some things he was never able to get used to.

Once I had been washed, he would recite simple sums and expect me to know the answer, whilst slathering my face in cocoa butter. 'So, Boobie,' he'd ask, 'what is 4+1?', his butter-like Bajan accent making the sound of the 'one' extend into the question mark. (Boobie was his pet name for me. It was once Boo-ga-loo-ga but over the years he had shortened it, thank God.)

From the very beginning, I knew it pleased him for me to show him that I was smart. So, without hesitation, I'd answer his sums between his soft caressing of my now very well moisturised cheeks.

As a black man who was part of the Windrush generation, my grandad was hell-bent on believing that anything could be achieved through hard work and a high level of education. His thoughts were not unlike most of the men of that era. It had been harder for him; he had been raised by a single mother in Barbados. Even the most idyllic of holiday destinations are someone else's home and potentially their hallway of hardship. He found sweet relief in his other four siblings and the freedom afforded to him by growing up against such a nature-rich backdrop, but there was more emphasis put on paying work than schoolwork. It was a lot later in my life that I would work out that he was extremely dyslexic. Often as a young girl, I would see him make excuses when it came to having to sign for something, or blaming his delayed understanding on his 'bad eye'. And yet, he was the one who encouraged me to 'flash my pen' when I wrote so that anyone observing me would know that I was serious.

What he lacked in his ability to read and write, he made up for by being a wonderful homemaker. In the late 1980s into the early 90s, long before men lobbied for equal paternity leave or made social media videos illustrating their efforts at learning about the 'emotional labour' often laid on their female counterparts, there was my grandad bucking the trend. An accomplished chef, his ability to prepare lavish meals at a moment's notice was unmatched. Soups, stews and heavily seasoned meats which were left to marinate in old ice cream tubs (which were now reserved for this sole purpose) overnight almost made the dining table bow under their bountiful weight, not just on Sundays but every day of the week.

He would keep a watchful eye on the laundry basket, sporadically asking my nan or mother if there was something specific they needed for work which would perhaps need to be dried quickly. When it came to cleaning, he moved like an artist. His duster was his paintbrush moving gracefully over the twenty or so random ornaments which, like most Caribbean homes of that time, would be artfully scattered across the living room – a place I was very rarely allowed to sit in, like most children. He took pride in creating a warm, clean and inviting environment that would be ready for visitors at a moment's notice, of which there were many. Both he and my nan were popular people. Like most Caribbean immigrants, they relied heavily on their new-found friendship circles to help keep homesickness at bay. Most Fridays 'uncles' and 'aunties' would fill the living room, and the soft slap of dominoes and deep, small island, accent-tinged laughs would provide the soundtrack to my sleep.

During my early years at nursery and primary school, he was always there at home time to collect me. Bentley was a firm believer in two things: dark rum and his dark-wood pipe. He would always be reaching into the left inside pocket of his Del Boy coat and pulling out an ochre-coloured pack of matches. In one movement he would strike the match, light his pipe, take three pulls and return the pack of matches to his pocket. As I ran from the classroom and into the playground, all I had to do was look for a body whose head had been replaced with a cloud of smoke. Once the smoke had cleared, there he was; not quite alienating himself from the mothers around him, but standing far enough away to make it clear that he didn't want to be bothered.

He was the original Mrs Doubtfire at a time when he was criticised for taking on the roles usually attached to the matriarch. Some of those closest to him found his willingness to do what the world saw as the more 'feminine' duties as something to be mocked.

'Come on now, we all know who wears the trousers! And it ain't Georgie!' a male family friend laughed one evening. 'If we really want to know how things are going to go, then I think it's best we ask Vern!' he added. The entire living room chuckled as if agreeing in unison.

He had a fair point. Vern really was a no-nonsense woman who took pride in dotting every 'I' and crossing every 'T'. Where my grandad excelled in making sure the house was kept together, my nan was meticulous about ensuring that there was, in fact, a house to be kept. Whilst she wasn't against having a tidy home, my nan wasn't as strict about cleaning as grandad was. That wasn't her thing. Her thing was balancing the books. Every Saturday morning before heading to the market, she would lay out every bill and IOU on top of their bed. Sitting on a dark oak ottoman, she would use a calculator as she looked through one of her many cheque books, ensuring that all the numbers made sense. When it came to money there wasn't a penny nor pound that got past her. Not only was she good at managing what they had, she was also a brilliant saver, making sure to put money aside for a rainy day – and monsoon season.

I often describe her as an oak tree: her roots are deep and unseen, perhaps entwined around memories too hard for her to share; her trunk is rigid and thick, unmoved by any metaphorical or actual upset that may blow her way. She is human, of course, and very rarely you might see her branches gently bend in the breeze. But note I said bend: I've yet to see one break.

But this is not to say that she didn't have a softer side; she did.

In fact, many would often remark that it was I who brought out that part of her personality. Although she worked during the week, Saturday and Sunday afternoons were usually reserved for her carting me to and from her friends' houses or to one of the many functions she had been invited to. In my earlier years it was almost unheard of for her to go anywhere without taking me along. On Friday evenings she would go through my wardrobe, sometimes allowing me to choose what dress and matching shoes I would sport that weekend. And her face would pop with pride whenever someone thought she was my mum.

'She looks just like me, doesn't she!' she laughed, clearly tickled that she still looked young enough to have such a young child. 'But no, I am her grandmother!' she would assure them, leaving a slight gap after announcing this to allow those she was in conversation with to interject with animated surprise and questions about her skincare routine.

After which she would always give me the tightest hug and let them know that I was her 'number one'.

And I was. Being her first and only grandchild, she always made me feel special. Nothing was too much trouble. When I began to show an interest in dance, it was she who found a nearby dance class in Streatham. She encouraged me to practise ballroom and jazz by not only paying for the thrice weekly classes but making sure my dance kit was always in tip-top condition. To this very day, one of her many treasured artefacts is a plastic rainbow. It might look like another useless ornament, but upon closer inspection you will see that inscribed across each colour of the rainbow is the name of a specific ballroom dance, like the cha-cha-cha or foxtrot. This was my award.

Every six weeks, we would be tested on a specific dance and if you passed, you were gifted with that portion of your rainbow. Of course, there were many times I found the choreography too difficult. Whilst I knew where my left foot should go, I struggled to get it there in time.

'You! You can dance!' one jazz teacher remarked during a dance lesson a decade or so later. 'But you struggle to pick up choreography and that will be your downfall,' she went on. It felt like the metaphorical sweet she had just given me had suddenly turned bitter. And not long afterwards, I gave up my long-held dream of being a professional dancer.

But back when I was a child, my nan would hear nothing of the sort. Each week we would arrive at the lesson and she would pull out her knitting. Her eyes would dart back and forth from her dancing needles to me whilst I stumbled ungracefully through a dance of my own. Some lessons would end in tears.

As we would make our way back to her car, she would hug me and tell me to try harder next time, but she would never agree to me quitting the classes altogether. Her balance between ensuring that I understood the importance of sticking to a goal but also leaving space for my childish frustrations was exactly what I needed at the time, even if I didn't know it. And it was a joy to waltz in those softer moments with her, because I knew that by the time we returned home any such gentleness would evaporate. My nan's mood mimicked her surroundings; when the house was quiet, her smiles were rare and any signs of happiness on her face were fleeting. I was wise enough to decipher that she and Grandad weren't getting along well, so maybe that was why.

Now I'm older, I get it. The Black Woman is one with many faces. This is not because we want to fool the world, but because we must work overtime to ensure the world doesn't fool us. Kindness can quickly be taken for weakness, and should a frown be worn for too long, the Black Woman could incorrectly be perceived as angry. But my nan cared not for the latter. She wasn't angry, she was busy. And perhaps she thought there was not much time for smiling as there was so much work to be done. She was simultaneously trying to save her home and marriage. That would suck the joy out of me too.

When I look back now, I think she busied herself with the more traditionally masculine aspects of the household because deep down (and publicly) she felt that she had stumbled into a life she never wanted. She was one of fourteen children born to less than happy parents, in what was often described as a house of horrors. It was clear that her own upbringing was quite the turn-off in regard to being a mother. 'I really wanted to be a nurse,' she told me, her soft Bajan accent pulling in on the words. 'I could've done so much with my life, but before I knew it, I had your mother, and shortly after, your uncle. Your grandad always wanted a big family, but I wanted to be free of the torture of home and build a life for myself.'

The first time I fell pregnant, she was forthright with her advice: 'If you know what's best for you, my dear, you better get rid of it.' She wasn't optimistic about the father, either. Even though I was no longer with him, once I had told him I was pregnant, he showered me with promises. And even though my then full stomach knew those promises were empty, I couldn't help but sometimes daydream about this perfect family set-up which I knew he would never deliver on. My nan was my instincts personified.

'Listen,' she warned. 'He is going to tell you all manner of things right now, but the minute that baby is born, you will be lumbered and stuck. You don't want to end up like your mother.'

That last line came at me like a sharp uppercut from Muhammad Ali himself and firmly boxed me out of my daydream and into the real world. My mum had all three of her children with the best intentions. Those intentions had been pumped with verbal steroids by, at the time, seemingly good men, but as the years had unravelled, she had been left holding the babies and the bills. My nan was right. I had been on the frontline of that struggle, and I didn't want to repeat that kind of history. Over the next few days it wasn't just the incorrectly named 'morning sickness' keeping me awake at night. I went back and forth with my decision over and over in my head, playing out each and every scenario I could think of.

My mum didn't even try to entertain the idea of an abortion.

'Babies are a blessing!'

'Anything that comes your way, we will work through it.'

'Life can change in twenty-four hours, and what feels like a struggle now could turn out to be your biggest success.'

Whilst I knew she meant well with her positive platitudes, I also knew that the time just wasn't right. Plus, it's easy to talk positively about hardship when hindsight is on your side. No encouraging words were enough to erase the nights when the lullaby to send me to sleep as a little girl was my mother's crying, because she was unsure of how she would pull off another week of raising us.

My mind was made up. I would have an abortion.

As geography would have it, the local Marie Stopes was a stone's throw from my nan's home. A four-minute walk, in fact. Nan was present when I made the initial call. My hand was shaking so much the phone's receiver was clanking repeatedly against my large earring.

'I'm sorry, love, can you repeat that?' the kind receptionist asked.

I made an appointment and hung up the phone.

A few days later I sat with an even kinder nurse who explained the various procedures available to me. After very little thought and even less research, I decided that the abortion pill was the best choice for me, but I was little prepared for how horrific this form of medical abortion – as it's termed – would be. I would have to take two tablets. The first would offer me the liberty of changing my mind. A few days later I would return and take the second pill. That pill was the end of the line. There would be no going back after that.

I swallowed the first pill with no hesitation, and then waited for a wave of guilt or a feeling like I was making a bad decision to hit me during this period of grace. It never came. So, with that, I decided to see it through to the end. By the time I had walked back to Nan's house after the second visit, the light tightenings in my tummy (which I now understand to be labour) were growing stronger by the second. Suddenly I had the urge to use the loo.

Bracing myself in the tiny toilet of my grandparents' home, I cried out for my nan.

'Nannnnnnnn!' I wailed, sweat dripping from my face.

The pain was all-consuming. I was barely eight weeks pregnant at this point. Even through the rolling tides of cramps that were forcing me to double up, I wondered how on earth women gave birth some seven months later and survived, if this was the level of pain I was in now.

'Nannnnnnnn!'

I heard her bounding up the stairs and she didn't flinch when she saw that her toilet now resembled a scene from *The Texas Chainsaw Massacre*. There was blood everywhere. I felt dizzy and discombobulated. I knew the smart thing was to remain seated on the toilet, but the amount of blood I was losing was so significant it felt as if the toilet wasn't going to be able to contain it all.

'Right, I am going to lift you into the bath,' Nan said, sweeping one of my arms around her neck and hoisting me into the bathroom next door.

'Listen,' she said sharply, as the tears cascaded down my cheeks, 'I know it's scary. But trust me, the worst will soon be over.'

And as she looked me dead in the eye, in that moment the connection was undeniable. She had never before mentioned choosing to have an abortion herself, and up until this day she has never confirmed it. But her swift thinking and rare moment of tenderness leads me to believe that such actions can only be rooted in experience.

So that was the end of my first pregnancy. The second time around, I didn't need a blue line to confirm that I was pregnant. My body just knew. It's hard to explain to those who haven't been pregnant, but before my belly ballooned or the constant feeling of being on a boat overtook me, there was no doubt in my mind that I was with child.

For some reason, this time around I felt very protective of the cluster of cells that had begun to develop within me. Nervous as I was, I knew that there was no way I could have an abortion for the second time, and I didn't want my nan's or anyone else's opinions trying to sway me. I barely had enough energy to make it through the day without feeling like I wanted to take a nap. I didn't have enough in the tank to take on the shoulda-woulda-coulda's of anyone else. But in true Vern fashion, she could sense when something was different, and when she asked me outright if I was pregnant, like a child who had been accused of their wrongdoing, I broke at the first poke.

'I knew it,' she said, as she stirred her tea. 'I dreamt of fish, you see. Whenever I dream about fish, someone around me is going to have a baby.'

Whilst the common use of spirituality can be a tad over-whelming and quite frankly hilarious to those outside the walls of our community, I have learned to believe in things like dreams having meaning and the bad 'juju' of others.

Like I say, this time I didn't have an overwhelming sensation to not become a mother. Nothing within me screamed that this would be the end of my life. There were no sirens or tinkering alarms. And that was something I had to pay attention to. Something within me told me that if I moved forward with this pregnancy, everything would be OK. Even though I knew my nan – and many others – would perhaps be disappointed. I think for both her and my grandad, I had felt like their second chance at parenting. They had cared for me as if they were my mum and dad, and neither one of them hid the fact that they had high expectations for me. Whilst no one said it out loud, I knew the fact that I had turned my back on university to go and travel had left a bitter taste in their mouths. Again, to them, education, in the most traditional sense, was everything. They had poured all they had into me, and the unspoken agreement was that I'd at least give them a picture of me in a cap and gown so they could show it off to their friends and boast about all I had become. Instead, the road I was on would lead me to wearing a medical gown too soon instead. My decision meant that I was charging full speed down a path beset with problems which would lead to me fighting to survive rather than thrive.

But for what it was worth, I knew there was one woman I could wholeheartedly depend on to support my decision to become a mother, and that was my own.

Junnie, or Jay as she is more commonly referred to, is perhaps the happiest bearer of children I have ever met. She assures me that long before she fell pregnant with me, she believed that her life's sole purpose was to have children and not much else. She dreamt of nothing more than being a mother. In fact, she dreamed of having five children. In reality, three of those wishes were granted. I am the eldest of three children and there are seven years between us all which means that all three of us are from different generations.

When my sister was born, the only pronounced and memorable feeling I can remember was one of overwhelming jealousy. My seven-year-old self was livid. How dare this tiny thing intrude on the most blissful relationships that I'd been the centre of for almost a decade? I don't think my relationship with my sister's father, who was soon to be my mother's husband, helped. Although I was young, I could tell that he wasn't all that he proclaimed to be. And it wasn't long after they said 'I do' that I realised why. That period of life is one I think I've chosen to forget as it was filled with the sharp staccato of smashing glass and the hushed voices of policemen.

And by the time he and my mother got married, Nan and Grandad's marriage had dissolved. It was a fallout which had been years in the making, and whilst I loved them both very dearly, they were better off apart than together. The love they had for me was stronger than the love they had for each other. It's far too conceited to think that me being removed from their care was the cause for the divorce, but I'm confident that I was the last thread of love tethering them together. For years they had perhaps used me as an excuse to overlook the lack of love within their union. But once I was out of the picture, it became clear that they could barely even look at each other.

With some of his money from the divorce proceedings, Grandad gifted Mum with the deposit for a three-bedroom house in West Norwood. It all seemed so exciting at first. We had spent a few years renting a two-bedroom flat in Crystal Palace. I had been bounced around between my mum's, my grandparents' and my father's, and now there was a new house all ready for us. Mum was heavily invested in creating the most beautiful environment for us, even if my new stepdad could not be bothered. My mum bought the house off a very old man whose wife had recently died, and the interior of the house hadn't been touched since the early 1940s. It was like stepping into a museum. The busy wallpaper induced an instant headache and the lime-green carpet was tacky with years of grime.

Mum and Grandad wasted no time in gutting the place, and within three months it had been turned into nothing short of a show home. I think by then Mum was already doubting the strength of her own marriage. She was working night and day as a sales manager to not only pay the mortgage but pay for the renovations. Her husband was doing the bare minimum of holding down a job as a security guard, being sure to go and play cricket on Saturdays and always having rice and peas with a banana for dinner. I really didn't like him, and even though I was so young, I wondered how long Mum was willing to ignore that he was never going to work as hard as her. I give her props, as she held on for longer than most, but when a family friend who also went to the same cricket club as my stepdad came round to tell Mum that he had been cheating once again, and this time he had the cojones to bring the woman to the cricket club whilst Mum was out at work putting in extra shifts, that was the last straw. Mum had finally been ready to face the fact that her husband was a serial cheater and the home that she had been struggling to build was not standing on a rock but on sand.

By the time the marriage had come to a welcome end, I

was eleven years old and I was mature for my age, so I had already slipped into the role of a mother's help as she worked late hours to desperately try and keep our family home afloat. It was my duty to collect my sister from school, as her nursery was on the way home, and look after her until my mum got home. Grandad was now living what felt like a world away in East Ham, but twice a week he would come and visit, and try to take pressure off of my mum. If it weren't for the alarming differences, I could have almost been tricked into believing that it was the good old days. There was no better feeling than returning home from school and being able to smell the scent of my grandad's pipe from the gate. Immediately my shoulders would relax, because I knew for at least the next forty-eight hours, I would be allowed to be a child. But when Grandad couldn't make it up there, I had to embrace my role as caregiver and protector for my younger sister.

Whilst my mum was at work, I was given strict instructions not to answer the door to anybody and be sure not to spend the entire evening glued to Nickelodeon. I can't remember being mothered during this period. I stopped letting her know about things like parents' evenings and school performances as I instinctively knew she had enough on her plate. I do remember once trying to convince her that she was leaving it too late to apply to secondary schools for me – my other school friends had by now already attended a handful of open days and had started taking entry exams. But to no avail. Basically, my mum was so overwhelmed by the changes in her life that, aside from struggling to keep me clothed and fed, the other stuff didn't matter.

At the end of every school year, there was a church service dedicated to congratulating the Year Six students and wishing them well on their educational journey once they had left the school. One of the most talked about moments in this service was when each child walked down the aisle to be presented with a Bible, and the head teacher read out which school they would be attending next. That evening I shook with shame because I knew what was coming.

As I made my way down the same aisle my mother walked down to get married, I kept silently begging that our head teacher wouldn't say anything at all. But she was a stickler for routine.

'Next we have Candice Brathwaite. Whose next school is . . . unconfirmed.'

I felt the soft wave of shame and sadness sweep over the congregation, and I hurriedly snatched my Bible from her with not so much as a thank you, before taking my place amongst the students already on the stage and trying my best not to cry.

When my brother was born, I was fourteen years old. When my mum fell pregnant with him, I was already doing just as much for my sister as my mother was, so when she told me she was expecting, I think I was subconsciously gearing myself up to take on even more responsibility. An older student was sent to come and find me in the middle of an English lesson to tell me that my mother had gone into labour. I knew what to do, leaving school immediately without even seeking permission from our stern Jamaican headmistress, and made it to Guy's and St Thomas' Hospital just after my mother had undergone an emergency C-section. The weight of my brother's tiny life left me breathless. Surely this would work out, I prayed.

But it wasn't the case for his father and my mother either. Once my brother was born, he was out more than he was in and it really took a toll on my mum once again. I remember my nights being broken by the sound of both the baby and my mum crying. Now I'm older, I can only imagine how deeply this period of her life affected her.

So used to doing what I could to ease her stress, I committed to helping her with some of the night feeds and bathing my brother once I'd come home from school. As with my sister, I became a permanent mothering fixture in my brother's life as he grew up. This, I have found, is not a unique experience. Many eldest children of single mothers find that very early on, their childhood experience is put on the back-burner or even eradicated altogether to make room for the premature parenting of their younger siblings.

As much as I loved my sister and brother, this experience is one of the most prominent reasons why, for many years, motherhood wasn't for me. I'd already done my bit and missed out on so much – all those extracurricular activities and birthday parties, for a start. Yes, these things would probably have not amounted to much more than me getting grotesquely drunk whilst thrusting my backside into the nether region of a young boy who was probably no good for me, and then getting hickeys, but that doesn't mean I should've skipped that part of my adolescence altogether. But as I looked upon my two younger siblings as my own children, I couldn't not be there for them. And those around me shared that view too. My own grandparents would often jokingly refer to me as my siblings' mother and up until this day, should my eighteen-year-old brother get a touch out of line, our mum will call me to see if I can verbally discipline him.

And whilst I'm being honest and open, I have to say that although I have no doubt my mother loves myself and my siblings dearly, I do view her more as a big sister rather than a mother figure, primarily because I spent too much of my youth parenting her through her battles with mental health. She had been diagnosed with depression in her early teens and has been on antidepressants most of her adult life. I had only been privy to her trying to self-harm once, but that was enough to remind me that anything could be a trigger. So, I had to develop this graceful balance between showing her respect as my mother but also knowing when it was time to show her tough love and gather her as if I were her sister or friend.

It wasn't only my own personal experience which had put me off motherhood. There were general stereotypes and beliefs directly projected onto black women that I just wasn't here for. One of these is the old 'mammy' narrative. During the times of legal slavery – just because it's illegal doesn't mean that slavery has come to an end – white women didn't just use their black female slaves as their handmaids, but as stand-in mothers too. The white wives of slave owners were usually much too preoccupied with fancy parties and social climbing and had no time to tend to their own babies.

So, guess who had the 'luxury' of becoming 'mammy'?

That's right. Black female slaves.

Images of black women 'wet nursing' white babies have become an iconic thread in the tapestry of womanhood and motherhood woven within slavery. Imagine the sheer horror of being raped every day, falling pregnant through an act of sexual violence, and then having that baby ripped from your arms and bosom only to have another infant – a white infant – put in its place.

And then with the abolition of slavery came a rejig of the visuals. All of a sudden, white women were consumed with all things wife and mother, and the black women who had lent them bond and breast were now outcast from a stage in womanhood of which they were the blueprint. Over the decades, the expectations set upon black women changed. Whilst slavery was now illegal, 'help' in the fifties and sixties was in vogue, and my grandmother's generation was still expected to mother their own children, pat the backs of their own husbands and then sleep long enough to be able to get up and tend to the homes and children of white women too. However, the white women employing black women at this time would not stand for their version of perfectly preened motherhood to be undermined in any way.

The ways in which we disciplined children, which once was a gift to the white mother, whose children we raised, like ours, with firm manners and an even firmer hand, were now deemed as abusive. The things we taught our children, which used to be fine for the pickneys of our masters – because they knew they would be skills that they could perhaps encourage their child to then use against us – were now not allowed in any kind of parenting programme.

And then, aside from the threads of our history which sought to strangle my idea of motherhood, I also couldn't ignore the inevitable culture clash which lay ahead. The father of my then unborn baby, Bode (pronounced like Beyoncé), is of Nigerian heritage, which was a 'big problem'. It was one thing to have a casual tryst with one, but to actually proceed in trying to build a family with someone from Nigeria was an absolute no-no.

For those who are not acquainted with the racial preju-dice within the black communities, as recently as two decades ago it was not yet a common thing for Africans – more specifically, West Africans – and, to be precise in this case, Nigerians – to 'go with' Afro-Caribbeans. For as long as I could remember, there was no insult as heavy with disrespect as being called or likened to a Nigerian. In a time before

Burna Boy, the Internet, and the general understanding and deep belief that all black people originate from a country in Africa, the war that raged between West Africans and Caribbeans specifically was potent and persistent. And from what my husband tells me, Nigerians were just as bad at upholding the false belief that they were somehow better than, and separate to, Caribbeans. He was taught that Caribbean people had no experience in building long-lasting relationships. His own parents warned him not to go halves on a child with a woman who would inevitably want to become a baby mother. And my family often wondered if he had only taken a liking to me so he could secure a British passport. Because, if we went by the way Nigerians were routinely portrayed, it meant they were only good for two things: marrying women to secure permanent residency within the UK, and using someone's credit card details to buy Grey Goose in the club every Friday. Like I said, unless you've lived it, it's hard to get your mind around.

But here we were, a modern-day Romeo and Juliet, quite frankly head-over-heels in lust and in love with each other, blind to these incorrect, negative stereotypes that had been present in our lives for as long as we could remember. Most of our early days were spent laid up in bed completely consumed by an unrelenting, physical need to be on top of one another all of the time. He was unlike anyone I'd ever met. And I knew that his love for me knew no bounds.

I was going to keep this baby.

All well and good. But when faced with the evidence that my stomach was full with the beginnings of a life co-created in love, it wasn't that straightforward or simple for either of us. The road ahead seemed steep and peppered with boulders. I had seen first-hand that when it came to black motherhood, love was not enough. But, strengthened by my unwavering belief in the idea that I could perhaps do things in a way that made me feel like a success, something shifted in me and I knew that now, pregnant and happy, I didn't just want to focus on the things which would prematurely halt my motherhood journey. Instead I wanted to daydream about perhaps being the best mother possible. One who was more inclined to remind their offspring that I was their parent and not one of their 'little friends'. A mother they could ask countless favours from or borrow money from. A mother who would be in a position to offer up career advice instead of having to encourage the keeping of a mediocre job to help top up the electric meter. A mother that could get their child on the property ladder before they turned thirty. Shit, one could dream.

Something other than morning sickness was churning away at my insides, and I really wanted to see if I had what it took to nurture a human who would grow up proud of the path I'd created for them. And deep longing aside, whilst my first abortion didn't play on my conscience, and until this very day I remain confident in that decision, I didn't think I had the emotional wherewithal to go through that process again, especially because the father of my child was really great. He was a full-time-employed (albeit poorly reimbursed), stand-up guy who had put his love for me at the centre of all that he did, including going against his very Nigerian family's wishes that our relationship didn't materialise.

And so, in this way, I knew that whilst the road ahead wouldn't be easy, filled with more judgements than a court-house, something told me to give it a try.

I guess love will do that to you.

2

DESMOND'S

At the time of the 2011 census, almost 19 per cent of black households were made up of a single parent with dependent children. This was the highest percentage out of all the ethnic groups for this type of household. The next census is due in 2021.

Most pregnancy books seem to cater for a particular sort of pregnant woman, and do a good job of excluding others who don't fall into that category. In my experience – even though I was going through a natural phenomenon which, give or take, is pretty universal – as a black mother-to-be with my black partner and my black baby-to-be, I felt invisible.

Not only was I not represented on the pages of these books, I was, as in all other walks of my life during that period, subject to a set of assumptions and prejudices that some healthcare professionals didn't even bother to hide.

Take the doctor I went to see to confirm my pregnancy. Bode was at work, so I was there on my own.

'Right,' he said as I told him I'd tested positive in a pregnancy test. 'And the father?' He swung his eyes around the room, knowing damn well a man wasn't just going to fall through the ceiling.

I screwed up my face.

'He is at work,' I said, as the anger rose up in me like the flames on an open fire. I wanted so badly to give him a verbal tongue-lashing for asking me a question that I knew he wouldn't dare ask a white patient. But instead I sat there awkwardly answering his queries in regards to my last period and finally, even though you'd assume this would be the first and most important thing, how I was feeling.

The truth was, I wasn't surprised. I was ready for that.

We all are. Black women, that is. Especially if you've been raised in a space where at every turn even breathing whilst black could be viewed as a problem.

My own experiences and those of black women I know mean that we have a first-class degree in making ourselves small. It started way before the subtle microaggressions regarding the quickness with which we could change hairstyles (in eight hours black women can go from sporting a teeny weeny Afro to backside-grazing box braids) or the scent of our 'spicy' (read 'well-seasoned') reheated food escaping from the office kitchen's microwave. For better or worse, the idea that we should shrink ourselves usually began at home.

Elders would often chase children out of their living rooms or kitchens so that we were out of earshot of their adult conversation. I do agree that kids should be kids, and shouldn't get caught up with 'grown folk' business, but this hard and fast rule unfortunately worked both ways in that we were both not seen and not heard. My peers and I would clam up at the mere thought of having to report something to an elder, even if the consequences of harbouring a secret were potentially grave. Sure, it could be as trivial as not wanting to vocalise that you weren't really feeling like another weekend meal of Saturday Soup, but at the most horrific end, you wouldn't say if you were dealing with any kind of abuse. That was an internal issue. No one wanted to hear you, and if you could find someone who would, and then they went on to believe you, you were a very lucky child indeed.

And that's how most of us were raised. If our own families didn't think we had anything to say, then what lay beyond our homes? We were raised readily expecting the world in which we live to think so very little of us.

For as long as I can remember, from what I could see, being a black woman has always meant that you were there just to service and please others, be that your parents, your man, your children, or your employer. If we were to draw up our own eulogies, we would perhaps often struggle to define ourselves outside of the shadows of someone else.

This had repercussions in terms of our bodies and how

we presented ourselves once we hit puberty. In my personal experience and from talking to other black women, it's clear that many of us never got the chance to recognise or express our own sexuality in our own way, as it was almost always thrust upon us.

'Do you remember the first time a man noticed you?' a friend asked recently. Of course I did, and like all other black girls I knew at the time, I was well underage. I was thirteen, making my way home from school. My youthful breasts barely filled out my bottle-green jumper.

'Eh gyal, look ripe eeeee!' I heard a patois-laced shout as I hurried past a packed barbershop on Brixton's Cold Harbour Lane.

Shamed and frightened, I stared at the pavement before me and wrapped my arms around myself to make sure they hid anything I had going on.

When I got home, I didn't tell my mum about it for two reasons. The first is that I knew this was a regular occurrence for girls my age. I mean, it felt as if it were some twisted rite of passage. And secondly, I knew she would chastise me for not walking the long way round.

This type of harassment was something that my mother, her mother and her mother before her were also used to. And it was not unique to them. The non-verbal consensus within our community was that most men were born sexual deviants who didn't care for trivial things such as being 'legal'. As soon as your uniform changed from primary to secondary school, all bets were off and it was time for them to begin their game of grooming.

A black girl's sexual maturing and its subsequent exploration were usually played out within the confines of her community like a game of cat and mouse. If you were lucky enough to have an older brother, uncle or full-time father figure, they might be able to act as a deterrent for the ill-meaning men who were trying to persuade you – with promises of five-pound notes and, if you 'went there', new trainers – and then you could probably make it out unscathed. But for those of us who didn't have a male relative who was willing to quite literally patrol the streets and act as your permanent bouncer, then the risk of you getting caught in their web was high.

The first one of my friends to get 'caught' gave birth to her daughter just as she was sitting her GCSEs. When she finally admitted to us that her pronounced stomach wasn't down to the fact that we were now allowed off the school premises for lunch (and we all loved the local chicken shop), most of us were shocked. She had presented as being the most sensible amongst us. She too had taken on a mothering role early in her childhood, and so it completely confused me as to why she would want to dive head-first into really becoming a mother. It felt weird when our form tutor asked us to drop off her latest piece of coursework to the ward where she was being kept post her C-section. Perhaps it was youthful igno-rance, maybe it was a cover-up (more than likely it was the morphine), but our friend seemed unfazed, so we all followed her lead. And we, her schoolmates, would dash to the hospital after school to coo over the baby and make hollow promises in regards to being there for her no matter what, all the while clinging to the feeling that it could be any one of us next. At any time, the false whispers of a wayward man could caress our eardrums and create a fictitious life filled with the love and attention which we so desperately craved.

But we also knew – from our mothers and grandmothers and aunties and cousins – that whilst he would tell us he loved us and would be there for us no matter what, nine months later we would be left to give birth alone, with our friends coming to see us, with or without their own babies, carrying our schoolwork. My friend survived as most of us do. It wasn't easy. My brother was born around the same time as her daughter and even though my own mother was feeling the financial pinch of having another mouth to feed, anything that could be passed down to my friend we gave her. She worked hard at continuing her education and providing a stable home for her daughter, but she never minced her words with us. She admitted that whilst she loved her daughter, she wished she had done things differently. By now her daughter's father was well out of the picture and she had become almost nun-like in her refusal to allow herself to have another relationship with another man. Almost nineteen years later, her sole focus is still her daughter and I can't say that I blame her.

And that was life. It was our duty to accept the lurid comments from black men just like the women before us had. It was our duty to not come across as too 'fresh' or too 'brazen', as that would inevitably get you a name for yourself. It was our duty to reckon with the hormonal and physical changes which were maliciously ricocheting through our bodies. A not uncommon conversation in many households might have gone something like this: a mother is calling up to her daughter, who is maybe eleven or twelve.

'Shanice! Be sure to get some proper clothes on and look decent. Your uncle Alvin is coming round later and you know how he stares. Don't give him anything to look at.'

Most of my school friends were shortening their skirt hems as they transitioned into teenagers. By now they were being courted by men in their twenties and the adults around us who knew didn't bat an eyelid. There was a common acceptance that we were now ripe for the picking. And I was no exception. Although naivety had me tricked into believing that my skimpy outfits were feminist choices inspired by Destiny's Child anthems, they were a misjudged cry for attention from men who would ride me like a train and then promptly get off at the next stop.

The problem is, when you have this, combined with a general reluctance to share with your carers how the challenges that come with your new reality now affects you, there is a lot that can slip beneath the radar. And of course there are things that can just be buried, including sexual assault.

I didn't want to write this next bit. Number one, it pulls up my own trauma, and number two, I thought I could write a book about black motherhood without it. But, to be honest, I couldn't be more wrong nor more cowardly.

I cannot continually ask something of those who engage with whatever I put out there, if I'm not willing to go there myself. It helps that I'm currently in therapy and have a safe space where I can work through all I am going to tell you. But for those women who aren't that supported, this part of the book comes with a massive trigger warning. If you've been a victim of sexual assault, abuse or coercion, and you have not been able to identify with the root cause of your trauma and relinquish self-imposed blame, then please head straight to Chapter Three.

But for those of you who feel strong enough to either gain a deeper insight into how sexuality is usually framed for black girls who aren't yet quite women but in the eyes of society are no longer children and you've had the opportunity to deal with your own personal trauma, then let's get to it.

I was just about to turn eighteen. The night is etched onto my memory because it was the night before my birthday, and a group of friends and I decided to go out that Friday night to celebrate. Only two of us had driving licences, so we split up between two cars and ended up at a rave on the back of the Old Kent Road in South London.

We had arrived a little early, so to warm up both ourselves

and the dance floor, we ordered as much alcohol as the wages of our temporary jobs could muster and we got absolutely shit-faced. By the time I received a text from a guy I had met with only once and went to the cinema with, the letters on my phone screen were all jumbling together. But he wanted to be my saviour. Or at least that's what I thought.

'TEXT ME WHERE U R. I WILL CUM AND GET U. U CLEARLY DON'T KNOW YOURSELF.'

I remember me asking a less-sloshed friend to send him a reply.

I remember him coming to get me.

I remember one friend asking me not to go.

I remember my other friends saying the same thing.

I remember going anyway.

I remember asking him to stop.

I remember him telling me not to overreact.

I remember a condom.

I remember the weight of him on top of me.

I remember making it out of the house.

I remember that I'd forgotten a shoe.

I remember running past the Tesco on Acre Lane.

I remember trying to sneak back into my nan's house.

I remember taking an hour-long shower.

I remember my hand shaking whilst trying to do the make-up for my birthday party the next day.

I remember being sick on my cake.

Happy eighteenth birthday to me.

For years, I fought myself on this experience. I told myself that I was to blame. That I shouldn't have gone back to his house. That I shouldn't have drunk so much. That I had it coming. In doing so I underestimated the power that this experience took from me. How my sexual identity was tugged unwillingly from my own grasp and how I spent almost a decade trying to con myself into believing that I still held it in my hands. And how it was perhaps the root of my most destructive behaviour to come. I thought all of these things before the time of #MeToo.

And by experience, I mean rape.

There, I said it.

I also knew that this was nothing new or special. Every other black woman I knew had been sexually assaulted in one way or another. Often it would be by a family friend respectfully referred to as 'uncle'; very rarely it would be by someone thought to be a boyfriend or even husband. The only thing that these rapes and sexual assaults had in common was the silence surrounding them, which turned up the volume on the normalcy. And in my case, I went back to a man's house, alone. There wasn't a case at all. So I chalked that up as a bad experience and tried to move forward with my life.

Fast-forward to my pregnancy and back to where I started this chapter: the reason I was so angry with that doctor who questioned the whereabouts of my partner was because it triggered all kinds of personal emotions linked to my story and those of the women around me. And I suppose I should have been more understanding towards this doctor, who had absorbed what the media was telling him. The media works hard, whether deliberately or unconsciously, to erase black fathers from the narrative of black families. This has been the case since slavery, when it was customary to take black husbands away from their wives and offspring. But that is not all. Black male slaves were routinely raped in front of their family and friends. This act is now more commonly known as 'buck breaking' or 'breaking the buck'. Slave owners used sodomy as a weapon to strip black men of all their pride and masculinity. By forcing others to watch, particularly young sons of the victims, the owners ensured that other slaves would never revolt or become too troublesome.

The lengths taken to ensure that black men falsely believed they weren't able to protect themselves, let alone their own families, has found a way to weave itself into our modern-day thinking. So much so, that in the autumn of 2018, an AQA GCSE (9-1) sociology book was pulled from publication because it stated that Caribbean men are 'largely absent' from family situations. Now, if we look at the data at the start of this chapter, one could attest that the sociology book was purely telling the truth. But as with most things race related, it's far more complicated than that.

Of course, these are things I wouldn't personally notice until I was in my late teens. The most interesting thing was that it bore such a stark contrast to what I knew to be true in my own family. Although my parents had split up, my father was a permanent fixture in my life, and I benefitted hugely from his presence and influence.

From the age of two, I saw him on weekends, and for longer periods during the Easter, Christmas and summer holidays. A short man with a gap in his teeth, a dimple in his left cheek and one in his chin, he was, along with my grandfather, my world.

Of course, neither of them was perfect. They both enjoyed a tipple and whilst I wouldn't say my father struggled with alcoholism, I will say that he drank beer and smoked excessively. And whilst not unhygienic, he was terribly un-domesticated. But the one thing my two male role models had in common was that they both made me feel like I could do and be anything.

I have a particular memory of my dad that has stayed with me. It was a sticky summer's afternoon and we had cycled back from the local park. Our bikes were resting against the front of the corner shop at the end of Dad's road and he was reminiscing.

'You know, Cand,' he began, as he ever so slowly, too slowly, unwrapped my Strawberry Cornetto for me (he never called me Candice, just Cand, as if the last three letters had got lost in the post). 'When I was a young boy, I had dreams of being a writer. A sportswriter, in fact. But it just wasn't an option for me.' He sighed heavily as he handed me my ice cream.

As I took my longed-for lick, he smiled. 'But you,' he said, his voice coming back to life. 'You will be able to do anything.'

And on we walked with our bikes in tow. I have carried that moment with me forever: I've unwrapped the depth of it, as I've tried to live as he advised me to.

My dad was a wise man. It's not that he didn't have the skills to be a writer – he was a brilliant wordsmith. And it wasn't that he didn't have the support, as my paternal grandparents raised him up to believe in himself whenever they could. But out there in the world, I bet for a black boy growing up in the 1970s, he felt like he had as much of a chance of being a sportswriter as he did playing football on the moon.

And yet, even though he had endured a life far removed from what he'd wanted for himself, not for one minute did he lay his burdens and disappointments on my shoulders. In fact, as I grew up, and the remits of his parenting became more constrained – not just because I was maturing into a young woman he didn't quite understand, but also because I was beginning to learn about his flaws and mistakes, the biggest of which was cheating on my mother with a woman who then became his wife – he still worked diligently to remind me that whatever it took to make a young black woman succeed, I was already in possession of it.

'I don't know what it is about you, Cand,' he once said, squinting into the hot summer sun that enveloped us as we walked between the two solicitors' offices he worked in and where he had given me a part-time receptionist role. 'But you just have "it". Whatever that "it" is that they always talk about in movies. You've just got it. It's like you're covered in some magical dust. Gimme some, nah?!' He laughed and rubbed his shoulder playfully against my own.

It's not until a lot later in my life – and I mean perhaps in the last two or three years – that I realised how important and influential both my grandfather and father were when it came to encouraging me to be an independent woman with a strong sense of self and self-worth. But to be honest, I still fell prey to the world's idea of myself due to the fact that I spent most of my teen years being told to my face and back that I was unattractive, primarily by boys who actually looked so much like me they could have been my siblings. And this in turn meant that I never, ever thought about having children. Children were for pretty girls that men would like to marry. Children were for women who enjoyed cooking and the company of other women. Children were for women who hadn't been raped.

As for me, my pregnancy began to clear a dark haze that had followed me since my father's untimely passing, which had left me devastated. He died when I was twenty-one. I'd been living in Naples. His work colleagues called me and explained that the flu he'd complained to me about on the phone, a mere two days before, had killed him. Stopping in at Whipps Cross Hospital on the way to an Arsenal match, he had barely made it to A&E before he went into cardiac arrest. His flu had developed into sepsis and poisoned his blood, causing the shutdown of his vital organs. Apparently, he had put up a fight. I heard he kicked a doctor to the floor in a last-ditch attempt to stay alive.

But by the time I saw him, the only thing he was kicking was rocks. With my head hung low over his cold and moulted body, I couldn't quite believe my eyes. It was still him, and not him, all at the same time. The dimple in his chin was prominent despite the cotton wool filling that had been put in his mouth to give his face a 'fuller' look. His receding but trademark hairline gave way to the incision at the back of his skull which was untidily peppered with staples. His glasses sat atop his unmoving expression and if I squinted one eye and cocked my head slightly to the right, it looked almost as if he'd fallen into a deep sleep. He was cold and rigid with rigor mortis, but asleep all the same.

For years after seeing him in the chapel of rest, the loss of him rocked me to my core and I had nightmares most nights for the next half a decade. At the same time, any value I had in myself went up in smoke. The first man to ever love me without wanting anything in return was no longer here to help encourage a positive sense of self. And, of course, this played out into how I interacted with other men.

Then I met Bode. And with our baby, I was being asked to carry a life which reminded me how much I should value my own. I don't know if you believe in all that 'woo-woo' stuff, but I do. I can't help but think that the baby was the timeliest gift. A gift which I hoped both my love and I would be able to celebrate. Not just because I personally felt that being able to raise a child with both parents in the household would be more beneficial (only if they are getting along, of course), but also because I'd known the sting of emptiness that comes with the almost indescribable longing for a father figure, that you just can't quite get a hold of – whether it be death or something less permanent keeping the dad at bay. I wanted a *Desmond's* kind of set-up.

When I was a kid, other than the comedy show *The Real McCoy*, the only show my family watched religiously was *Desmond's*. Set in a barbershop based in Peckham, it centred around the fictional character Desmond Ambrose (played by Norman Beaton), who was the loveable father of a nuclear family. The show was a hit with everyone in the community. The steel-pan-filled theme tune aptly titled 'Don't Scratch My Soca' ran through my grandparents' house like a call-to-arms. Sang by Norman Beaton himself, even the lyrics – about warm nights, the ocean breeze, rum and coconut trees – were a gentle nod to the life my grandparents had left behind.

With lyrics like those, it was no surprise to see them so enamoured by the show. To see a black family unit not only displayed, but celebrated, was a big deal and I perhaps had no true understanding of what watching such a positive display of black love and a two-parent family unit did for my psyche. For half an hour every day, it reinforced the idea that this funny, chaotic and loving black family was the norm. And now, even though historians may say we have moved forward when it comes to diversity, inclusion and equality, why is it that I genuinely struggle to name a show as resoundingly black, British and positive as *Desmond's*?

More pressingly, why do so many black men feel it's OK to turn their back on their own children and leave women to try and take on the roles of both mother and father, but also have their own children wondering about not only who they are, but if they are even loved? It is here that I would like to say that I believe there are multiple variations of being a single parent. Those lucky enough (not that luck should come into it, but it's hard to find a more fitting word) to find themselves with a man willing to stand up to his responsibilities can often find some momentary respite in knowing that they can call on someone if the child's school shoes are too small or they need help with childcare. But the same cannot be said for those women who find themselves so alone in the act of child raising, as if they had fallen pregnant by immaculate conception.

Whilst I not only knew my father, and that he wanted and loved me, I've been close enough to feel the flames of pain and anger that emit from those who perhaps couldn't pick their fathers out in a line-up, and my heart goes out to them. From what I had witnessed, I never wanted to be left holding a baby alone. And more to the point, I had to assess, unpack and show gratitude at what having my father present in my life had done for me and my self-esteem, even if we were only able to spend twenty years together.

It was of upmost importance to me that I had a baby with a man who understood that being a single mother wasn't in my plans at all. And for better or worse, Bode understood that. Not just with empty words, but with actual action, as he already had a daughter from a previous relationship. From our first ever conversation, he made it clear that he was a father and that his daughter was his main priority. He gave me the necessary space to weigh up whether I wanted to embark on a relationship with someone who was already a father, and whose world I could never be the centre of, as another female already had that place. To be brutally honest, I wasn't sure. I had a terrible relationship with my own step-mother. I think it was primarily because my mere existence and the fact she was unable to have children for my father was a major bone of contention for her. She was the only example I had of a stepmother and I personally don't think she was a great one. I secretly worried that there was no other version of step-parenting other than what I had experienced, and initially I didn't want the responsibility of trying to be a part-time mother to someone else.

But as time went on and my love for Bode intensified, my doubts decreased. Even though, amongst girlfriends, most of us had sworn off dating a man who already had kids – to be able to dodge the Baby Mother 'drama' (how ironic) and any other baggage that came with rightfully playing second fiddle – watching him present himself as someone's proud father filled me with hope. I knew that should we decide to have children together, I could confidently say that he was up to the task and that made him all the more appealing.

Tall, dark and handsome?

Yes, yes and very yes.

But at a time when it felt that so many men who fit that description were falling short when it really counted, Bode's display of active and proud fatherhood ended up being the biggest check against his name.

When I went online recently and spoke about having a supportive partner, I was shocked to see that there were quite a few comments suggesting that I hadn't got lucky, I just had great judgement. I personally couldn't disagree more. Having had my ear on the receiving end of many a man's sweet nothings, I have had first-hand experience of almost getting swept away by a slick talker. In the heat of the moment, it's so easy to do so. Cause you know, some men are like bags of spinach. Plump and full when you first pick them up, but once brought to boiling point, there isn't much there at all. I don't think women, of any race, should then be left holding not only the baby, but also society's twin favourites, guilt and shame, because a man wasn't one of his word.

Let's be honest, I have yet to meet a woman who knew that the man she chose to have a kid with would end up acting like a child himself, unable to face up to the new adult task placed in front of him. But for black women in particular, the actions of those boys have more costly societal repercussions. The concept of a woman as a Baby Mother isn't born, it is created. Its conception comes from the fact that a boy chose to not be a man and do his duty as a father, and as a result people frown upon a woman just doing the best she can with the cards she has been dealt.

With that said, I was going to have this baby with Bode. Hopefully the cards would be in my favour.

3

SECURE THE (BABY) BAG

*'Children from Black and minority ethnic groups
are more likely to be in poverty: 45 per cent
are now in poverty, compared with 26 per cent
of children in White British families.'*
(Child Poverty Action Group, 2019)

It's a universally accepted fact that people would far sooner admit to catching chlamydia after a quick tryst in Napa than reveal their credit scores. But in the black community, in my opinion and from the conversations I've had, there seems to be an extra lock and key on any discussion regarding finances – and especially how to manage them. I have butterflies in my stomach as I write this, because I feel like I won't just be lifting the lid on my own relationship with money, but also, it feels to me, on the secret garden of how an entire community has been taught – or, perhaps more fittingly, not taught – to deal with money. But, if by sharing my own experience, I may do some good and help other mothers to be better prepared for the task ahead, then the exposé will be well worth it. And also, I just don't see how I could possibly discuss motherhood and, in turn, parenting, without exploring the one thing that makes the difference between a buoyant upbringing filled with extracurricular activities and one where there's no guarantee of food on the table.

Of course, I can't speak for all black people, but of those I know personally, none – I repeat, not one of them – had planned to have children, and like almost everybody, Bode and I certainly did not feel as though we had the financial wherewithal to have a child.

When I listen to the motherhood journeys of those who come from a more privileged section of society – a society which seeks to raise them up, instead of tear them down – I'm always so surprised about how orchestrated it all seems to be. Or how possible: these women dare to imagine they'll be in long-lasting relationships, that they might be able to carry on with their careers thanks to the help of a nanny or an au pair; they're even assuming that their children will grow up and go to university.

When I was young, all of the routes available from where I stood that led to motherhood never seemed to include 'meeting a cute lad at uni' or 'having a well-paid career'. To be frank, most black women trying to raise children, whether in a relationship or alone, all seemed to need to get a payday loan on top of their pay cheque to see them through.

As for me, until I met Bode, I'd only ever interacted with men who had taken from me. Some were sweet and others were violent, but their desire to steal – be it confidence or actual coins (one time, I caught the guy I was dating lifting twenty pounds from my purse when he thought I was sleeping – I never confronted him about it) – was always the same. So even though now, on the face of it, I appeared to be with a man who loved me dearly and who claimed to be invested in both me and the life of our unborn child, my heart slept with one eye open, always ready to have to get on with raising a child alone.

In the days after realising I was pregnant, one of my biggest worries, other than the general health of the unborn baby I was carrying, was how we were going to feed it. Bode and I seemed to be living from hand-to-mouth, which was fine when it was just us and we were having too much sex to worry about hunger pains. We were young and in love, and being poorer than most just seemed to be a given at that stage of our lives. But such youthful ignorance and optimism was not going to fill the stomach of a hungry baby, and so it was time to face the music.

We owned nothing but dreams, and as poetic as that may sound on paper, the penny-pinching reality made me feel really uncomfortable. Even though I was still conflicted about whom to share this news with first, there was one person I was happy that I wouldn't have to broach the subject with: my dad, because he'd died four years previously. You see, he really believed in sensible pre-planning. Whilst he wasn't able to configure his own life to replicate that exact template, the things he advised me to do informed me that it was what he had at the very least hoped for me and, at best, expected.

'Don't be suckered in by these young boys, Cand,' he'd warned one summer's day, shooting a look at the almost-see-through maxi dress I was wearing. 'You want to finish school and secure a good job before getting drawn into any of that mess.' He gesticulated to a crowd of boys on bikes who weren't necessarily causing any harm but didn't look like they were up to any good either.

'Yes, Dad!' I giggled, embarrassed. We just didn't have that kind of relationship and I wasn't about to prolong the conversation so we could start now. He was the last man on earth I would talk to about any 'boy trouble'. Actually, I liked to have him believe that I had no interest in the opposite sex at all. Of course, nothing could have been further from the truth – I was a teenager, after all – but ever since he had lost his rag over an A2-sized poster of a bare-chested Peter Andre, which I thought I'd smartly positioned on the back of the bedroom door at his house, I promised myself that I wouldn't broach the subject of men until I was clean into my fifties.

As life would have it, I didn't get that chance.

I have no doubt he would have come to love Bode and shower his grandchildren with ridiculous things like those 'life-size' BMWs a kid can drive, teeny Adidas Gazelles and trips to see his beloved Arsenal play. But back then, when I fell pregnant – with my ever-expanding waistline and our ever-diminishing pockets – I think he would have thought I'd lost my damn mind. Like I say, he was always a man with a plan. And that is the one thing I didn't have. I knew that in his mind, I had deviated and pivoted far too much. Carrying this embryo, I was also carrying the misplaced guilt that I had somehow let him down. In a way, with his death, I had a narrow escape in having to explain myself. But if there was one thing I was willing to take from him, it was his pragmatic approach to the cards life deals out. I therefore spent hours on apps that allowed me to get an insight into how much it would take to raise a child to the age of eighteen. Once you threw in housing costs, the total amount usually consisted of six figures – and that was still the no-frills version.

Bode and I were both in full-time employment; at the time I was a receptionist on £8 an hour and Bode was on £17,000 a year in the tool hire industry. But no matter how I chopped, screwed and stretched, those figures were not turning our yearly take-home into six-figure anything. The calculator always came back saying the same thing: we were too fucking poor to have a kid.

The only upside was the size of our house. We were renting a three-bedroom place with a nice-sized garden from my mum, who had left her council property empty to go and live with her then husband. But there was a catch. Because even that silver lining, when put under a bright light, looked a little more like steel. Our housing set-up wasn't safe, and at any moment, Mum could want her house back. Then what?

Even though I didn't talk about my financial worries much, it was obviously on my mind, dancing around my subconscious like a never-ending nightmare. Every time I slept, I imagined the sweetness of my newborn's face until my dream was hastily interrupted by the harsh reality that we couldn't possibly afford what it would cost to give our kid the best start ever.

But the fact was, we were committed to having this baby and we would just have to find a way to make it work.

Maybe I felt it would be OK because that was what my mother's experience had been, and I'd seen up-close that things could be really tough, but still you just got on with it. I have to be frank: I wasn't born into poverty. By most standards, the lifestyle I had as a child – which was primarily funded by my grandparents – was one that most people would wish for. There were regular summer holidays back 'home home' to Barbados. There was always an abundant amount of food on the table. I even attended private ballroom lessons every Saturday (my other two lessons per week were group sessions). I didn't think about money or the stress it could bring until after my mother's divorce from my stepdad.

For reasons perhaps outside my mum's control, from the age of eight, the life I lived with her was very different from the one I had lived with my grandparents. The divorce meant that we were turned out of the family home. She wasn't able to cover the mortgage repayments as a single parent, so we suddenly found ourselves thrust into the rough grip of council housing. For those who have never had to be beholden to a very broken system, I encourage you to thank your lucky stars, because it is brutal. We moved home eight times in seven years until we were finally allocated a permanent home. All our homes before that were considered temporary housing. Some were very obviously uncared for and others weren't in the safest of areas. Finally being given the chance to unpack once and for all felt like a gift from God, I tell ya.

Still, money seemed to slip through her fingers. Bless her heart; maybe it was because she had too many mouths to feed or because she never had the correct financial advice, but either way, my mother just couldn't get a decent grasp on her purse strings. Bills would go unopened for fear of having to reckon with the fact that there wasn't enough money to pay them, and there were many hushed whispers as we hid in the bathroom because we knew that that knock, that was the bailiff. It was especially weird because, as I mentioned, I wasn't born poor. My maternal grandparents made it work one way or another, and until I was in my mother's sole custody. I enjoyed life in a way that I believe all children should: my greatest concerns involved acquiring the latest piece of plastic from Argos or working out how to make a friendship bracelet. But with the breakdown of my mother's marriage came the understanding that money ruled the world, and we just didn't have enough of it; so my world, as I knew it, just stopped spinning.

'What's for dinner?' I'd ask, shrugging my school bag off my shoulders and letting it fall to the floor with a thud. By now my baby brother had been born and Mum had no choice but to pack in work altogether.

'You know what it is,' Mum would answer, flatly.

Even though the answer never changed, and this meal always left me hungry, I enjoyed the way that, when I asked, hope filled my stomach for a few fleeting moments. But, alas, it was always the same: tinned salmon and boxed rice from Aldi or Lidl. Way before they were seen as the go-to spots for fashionably frugal millennials, they were places that could bring on more shame than not timing the change of a tampon right when wearing white. But at the time, that's where all our food came from. And whilst I look back and I am grateful to have gone to bed with a meal, I would have killed (a chicken perhaps?) for some variety.

Aside from those close calls with the bailiffs, my financial education whilst growing up had been pretty paltry. My nan and dad, the two wisest penny pinchers I knew, tried at every turn to encourage me to 'save', and bit by bit they introduced me to things like shares and ISAs, but beyond fleeting warnings to protect my credit and not blow my entire pay cheque in a few days, there was nothing else.

And now I was paying the price for that lack of education,

with the money I didn't have. Did I mention that one of my favourite songs is 'Ironic' by Alanis Morissette?

Conversations with various friends made it obvious that I wasn't alone in thinking that now would be an ideal time for the Bank of Mum and Dad to step in. After speaking with white acquaintances from middle-class backgrounds, it became very apparent that they often have a financial head-start that most black people I know could only ever dream about. According to research from Legal and General and the economics consultancy Cebr, in 2017 it was estimated that first-time buyers borrowed over six billion pounds from their parents that year alone. And yet according to a House of Commons report in June 2017, fewer than a third of black households are headed by owner-occupiers. The proof was in the pudding, as I knew of only one, yes, one friend whose mother had remortgaged her own home to help her daughter secure her first house. Most people I knew had nothing to remortgage, and the few who did seemed to have a hard time offering help to anyone, including their own children.

But this was cultural, too. I remember how furious my nan was when my grandad took money from their divorce settlement and gave it to my mum to use as a deposit to buy her first home – the home we consequently lost, but loved, regardless.

'I came to this country alone,' my nan explained, echoing almost everyone of her generation. 'And every little penny I made, I saved and saved. It was hard work. Now, these young people come by things too easy. If I had to work hour upon hour to make something of myself, they should have to also.'

That 'I suffered, so you will also have to' mentality wasn't uncommon. There seemed to be an unrelenting idea that there was a better chance to 'build character' when things were earned and not given.

After school, I threw myself into the drudgery of the working world to finance my insatiable need to travel the world. The fact my nan had introduced me to travel at such a young age meant that I was obsessed with being able to travel across the globe. At eighteen I was given the chance to live in India for two months via the now defunct charity Platform2. The idea behind the charity was to give young British people who were in no financial position to have a gap year of sorts the chance to travel. In return we would live and work locally, hopefully giving back to the community we were placed in. They were partnered with various countries, including Kenya, Ghana and Peru. When I was given the opportunity to sign up for the programme, it was all I could think about, even when I found out that I was going to be placed in India.

'Fucking hell, Cand, excuse my French,' my dad swore when I told him where I was headed to. 'Make no mistake, this is going to be a culture shock – but if you're not going to go to an actual university, you may as well get a degree in life experience,' he ultimately encouraged.

Would things have been different if I had gone to university? I doubt it. Bode had been to one, and whilst he was better paid, he was no further ahead on the career ladder than me. Looking at my friends who had gone on to higher education made it clear that there was a distinct feeling that they had been lied to. Most of them had degree certificates that their parents proudly displayed in glass cabinets (untouchable decorations of no use to anyone, quite like the degrees themselves), an overwhelming amount of debt and zero-hour contracts. At least I had memories, a full passport and an invisible scar where life thoroughly roughed me up along the way.

Despite the different paths we had all taken, what we did have in common is that none of us were even close to becoming homeowners. A few of us had struck gold and had been able to secure a council property at a time when most London boroughs had them going spare. But the overwhelming majority of us were still living at home, hoping that one day we would be able to scrape together enough money for a deposit, even though the help we provided for our extended families had a habit of swallowing most of our earnings.

Because there was another difference. Where most white students returned home to take some pressure off their purses, most of my black comrades were barely able to save at all due to the guilt that consumed both them and every pay cheque whilst living at home.

Being the eldest of three siblings to a single mother, I had been there before. A donation to the rent was standard practice and if you had the cheek to be employed full-time and didn't contribute up to half of your salary to the household you lived in, it would be considered seriously 'disrespectful'. And no talk peppers your ears or your social life more than what 'aunties' are saying about you:

'The house needs new sofas and no one else's credit is up to the task? You've got this.'

'The younger sibling needs a new school uniform and Dad is nowhere to be found? You've got this.'

'Want to have something else to eat even when you are told "there is rice at home"? You better have this.' Because no one else was going to supplement this sudden indulgent change in appetite.

And so, many of my mates and I were given the reverse of a head-start; we were screwed before we even began to create families of our own. Alongside these issues built into the community, we were being financially strangled by an infrastructure that wasn't built to encourage the financial literacy, let alone freedom, of black people. I had spent my late teens and early twenties working in service roles, like being a receptionist (which really needs to be respected more, to be honest; receptionists put up with a lot of shit), quite unaware of just how much upper-middle-class nepotism was helping advance the Bens and Billies I made tea for. I had always wanted a creative career – more specifically, to be the editor of a magazine. I wasn't picky, as I understood that I had to start somewhere, but if the images that I salvaged from fashion magazines were anything to go by, then I would say a career in fashion would have been the dream. But those careers required doing back-to-back unpaid work experience, and that wasn't even up for discussion. Whilst I knew it could potentially help take me one step closer to the profession I desired, it would obliterate any financial help I could give to my household, and so that dream had a premature heart attack and died. This wasn't a new thing. My mother recounts her own waiting on the porch on both her and her brother's payday when they started working. It was no use trying to lie about what they were bringing home either. Their wage slips had already been given the once-over. Remember, no penny nor pound got past my nan.

And now I was pregnant, so any more thoughts of trying to establish, let alone grow, a career came to an immediate halt, adding to my stress surrounding our lack of financial solvency.

There was nothing for it but to budget, and budget carefully. At least Bode and I had our 'own' home because of living as we did in my mother's council house. The monthly cost of rent and council tax combined was less than half of what it would have cost us if we'd had to rent privately. It wasn't perfect and it wasn't ours, but it beat paying someone else's mortgage for double the dollars.

This was the space our baby would come to know as

home. Luckily it was a three-bedroom property, so Bode and I agreed that we would do up a room as a nursery. I don't subscribe to the belief that you shouldn't seek to do up a home just because you don't own it. It's always been important to me that wherever I lay my head feels like a palace, so I had already painted various rooms and filled the space with second-hand pieces from the British Heart Foundation.

The idea of a nursery made me happy even if the thought of buying the necessary things like, you know, a cot and nappies, filled me with dread. But the plan was that I would breastfeed exclusively, which would save money. When people smiled and said, 'Yes, that's wonderful. So much better for the baby,' I just grinned and nodded. Truth be told, I could think of few things worse than having a mini-me permanently attached to my tit, but formula was a tenner a tin and I was worried that if the baby's appetite was anything like its father's, we would quickly be in the red. Food is a necessity, of course, but if there was a way to keep the overheads of a human being low, we were going to try and utilise it.

Despite the need to budget carefully and wisely, there was one item that I absolutely didn't want to be seen without. It was the mark du jour that supposedly represents the kind of mother you are before you've even introduced yourself; the item that acts as a megaphone, announcing what tribe of motherhood you belonged to.

The pushchair.

Now I'm not talking about any pushchair; this particular

brand was like the Lamborghini of baby vehicles. Its reputation was renowned, and its finish was spectacular.

The pushchair in question?

A Bugaboo, of course.

Before I had fallen pregnant, the only Bugaboo I knew was the hit song by Destiny's Child. Of course, I knew that babies required some kind of construction to be carted around in. I'd helped a few struggling mothers when they were stranded at one of the many train stations not equipped with lifts. But I'd never had any good reason to research pushchairs in depth.

Once again, the Internet wasted no time in reminding me that I was ill-equipped for the task of motherhood. Pages and pages of online forums remarked that the Bugaboo was not only the most stylish pushchair, but also the safest.

'I know they're expensive,' one online commentator began, 'but I couldn't imagine going for one of these knock-offs. Imagine if something were to happen to the baby? I would never forgive myself.'

Upon reflection, I now see how crazy this all was, but I'm also aware of how deeply rooted my anxiety to get it right was. When black people arrived in the Britain they were told was Great, all they had was the willingness to work and the clothes on their backs, clothes which were always well pressed and well cared for. And looking presentable had been drummed into me from an early age. 'If you don't have a pound in your pocket, your attire shouldn't show it!'

my grandad would recite each morning whilst fussing with the particulars of my school uniform. And of course my nan was slicker than butter on heat. Even though I had long outgrown wanting to wear matching dresses with her, she took her sartorial choices very seriously.

We were taught to be proud about how we looked, because the way we presented ourselves impacted on how we were treated by society. We didn't – and in many ways, still don't – have the luxury of not thinking about our outfits, because we instinctively know that we have to go the extra mile. So, when young black people are chastised for seeking designer garments before saving their money, I often want to stand up for them, as those who judge these choices don't seek to understand that there is more to it than wanting to be seen as 'cool' or 'on trend'. Being well dressed and in possession of the latest items was quite literally how black people were able to gain access to spaces that were usually closed off to them, not only for being black but also poor. And appearing to be financially solvent was quicker and cheaper than actually being so.

So, I admit that that is exactly what I was doing when trying to get my hands on a Bugaboo. I was trying to present myself to the world as having it all together. I was trying to say that no matter what people thought of me, I wasn't that. Look, look at my cute baby and thousand-pound pram. I don't care what you think about any other young black woman with a baby. If you took one look at me, your stereotypes would be shot to shit.

It wouldn't matter that we were renting our home.

Or that we often skipped lunch or dinner to keep food costs down.

Or that we piled on jumpers in the winter because the gas meter took every extra penny.

Or that date nights were spending fifteen pounds in Ikea.

Or that we purchased our mattress from a man with a van for seventy pounds.

None of that would matter as that's not what the world would see.

I knew that the 'mother' version of me would be judged before I even had the chance to introduce myself, so if being able to give myself and my baby a head-start meant getting my hands on a pushchair that made people believe that not only did I know what I was doing, but I also had the where-withal to get it done.

Deep down, however, I was panicking. Brand new Buga-boos weren't cheap. Despite searching high and low, the base alone was coming in at £800. Eight hundred fucking quid for what was essentially just four wheels and a hard seat. The carrycot, footmuff, basket and much-desired coffee-cup holder (let's be honest, I'd have to live on the stuff with all of the sleepless nights I had up ahead of me) were all sold as extras, bringing the final figure closer to an eye-watering £1,300.

'Oya! Are they mad?!' Bode yelled one evening when I presented him with the price. 'Come on now, will the pushchair get the baby into Oxford as well? Abeg, just carry the baby on your back until it can walk.'

'Or we can just send our money back home for someone's fancy wheelchair,' I shouted. He looked at me. We'd had a ferocious argument a few nights before over the amount of money from his salary that he sent 'back home'. There was so much we couldn't buy and even more we couldn't yet afford, and it drove me mad that he felt he had to send a single penny to his family, knowing we had a baby on the way. 'Candice,' he had yelled back at me. 'You wouldn't understand! It's culture.'

Of course I understood. Ever since I was little, I'd heard stories of older black folk having to send money 'back home', sometimes to an address they hadn't ever even been to. Even then, I understood that there was little sense in sending money backwards. The fact that a lot of those older relatives expected their children and their children's children to cater to them made me very angry. Why wasn't money being sent forward in the faith and hope that it could make their children's lives better?

'Babe,' he said now, his tone softening. 'I know it's tough, but you know we ain't got it like that right now. I'm not saying we won't in the future, but at this current moment, that piece of kit is outside of our budget.'

He was right and I knew it. Even if he didn't send any money back home, the cost of a new Bugaboo was way out of our reach, ridiculously adding up to be more than what we estimated we would need for the baby's first year.

My mum nailed it – and me – in one.

'I don't know about all of this,' she sighed, following me around John Lewis one damp afternoon as I gazed longingly at the brand-new, gleaming Bugaboos.

'But look at all the equipment,' I said.

She took one hard look at the accessories and a harder look at me. 'Footmuffs?' she said contemptuously, sucking her teeth. 'What's that? Nah, man. Back in my day, we just flung two blankets around the baby's legs and done. Don't fall for all of this hype. And an expensive hype at that.'

Hype. Hype that I had fallen hook, line and sinker for. I didn't have the energy to start reeling off why a Bugaboo was the best choice. But pretty soon, I'd have to face up to the fact that our pockets just wouldn't stretch that far.

I was becoming increasingly stressed by not having enough money to provide for our baby. 'I don't know if we can do this,' I admitted to my grandad one day. 'It takes a lot of money to raise a baby.'

'Now listen, kid,' he said, rubbing his chin in the knowing way only he could do. 'I know a thing or two about raising babies. I mean, I had a hand in raising you. And it ain't easy. But this I do know. You don't want to make a permanent decision based on temporary circumstance. Boobie, life is always changing. And you can be down today and up tomorrow. Imagine if you don't have this baby and you win the lottery tomorrow. You will never forgive yourself.' He wagged his finger to signify his seriousness.

I didn't want to put a pin in his positivity by telling him that I didn't play the lottery, so our money worries were not just going to evaporate overnight, but I did understand his sentiment. He was right. Who knew what tomorrow held? Life would figure itself out, regardless of my current headache.

That night I lay in bed determined to find my dream pushchair. I had listened to the advice of those who told me that spending so much on a buggy was a bad idea. I had to be more resourceful, find the answer, like my dad had taught me. So, I turned to the one place that would give me what I wanted for a far better price – and that magical corner of the Internet was Gumtree.

Gumtree was a godsend when it came to acquiring pieces for the home that were considerably outside of my price range. And aside from clothes (just personal preference), I saw very little wrong with getting second-hand items for the baby, even if it went against the continued belief in juju from both the Caribbean and African sides of my family.

'We don't know the spirit of the people who owned these things before you,' my mother-in-law pronounced.

'You're better than me,' a friend told me when I suggested Gumtree. 'I would have to wash tings three times in holy water before putting my newborn in it.'

I rolled my eyes at all of this well-meaning advice. All I wanted was a pushchair that I didn't have to pay through the nose for. And within a few hours, I'd found it.

SECOND-GEN BUGABOO CHAMELEON. GREAT CONDITION. £250 ONO. KILBURN LOCATION. COLLECTION ONLY.

I squealed with delight.

'What's up?' Bode asked, looking up from his laptop.

'Nothing, nothing,' I said hastily, not wanting to stir up suspicion.

Experience had taught me that I shouldn't run everything past him. He had already made it clear that he thought the price of such baby paraphernalia was a complete rip-off, and that we should 'cut our coats according to our cloth' and just go with the unbranded pushchair with the best Amazon reviews. But seeing as he wasn't going to be the one pushing this thing around the local mummy clubs, being judged before opening his mouth, I thought it best to not say anything.

I'd struck gold. Gumtree was overwhelmed with parents wanting to get rid of Bugaboo pushchairs left, right and centre. And although I was disgruntled that the baby would have to be given a hand-me-down, I abated that guilt by figuring that I was also being frugal and resourceful.

I emailed the seller immediately and made quiet plans about how I would retrieve it. We didn't have a car, so I would have to get a bus, three tubes and walk. That was fine. At least there was one part of this motherhood thing I could get right.

The day came to collect the second-gen Bugaboo. I was just shy of being five months pregnant. My sister had offered to accompany me. I was so tired, I looked past the fact that right now, next to her, I felt like Shrek. Usually, I scrub up well. Hell, at a push I think people are intrigued by my looks because my confidence pulls them in. But my sister is a classic beauty, no confidence needed. Being around her at this time was a reminder about all I had chosen to give up. She was studying at college and holding down a job as a sales assistant, and in between that she was doing what nineteen-year-olds do: meeting up with friends, taking ages to get ready and being blissfully unaware of how at any moment, life could slap her upside the head and decide to take her in a less carefree direction. Even though I was approaching a very unsure time of my life, I still felt very protective of her. As the tube rattled towards Kilburn, I became overwhelmed with emotion and had to fight back tears. In a more romanticised, popular version of this play, the mum and dad would spend hours in their local Mothercare before happily parting with an amount that could easily cover two months' rent. I had an envelope with £210 inside and my baby sister, who would offer physical help should I need it. Who the hell was I kidding? And I felt like a mess. But now wasn't the time to show it. The one thing I was proud of was having been able to bring the price down by forty pounds. Bode was a master haggler, so he would have appreciated my efforts. Even though I was most sure that he was going to throw a wobbly that I'd even gone for a name-brand pushchair in the first place, I knew that he would be slyly proud of me being able to make a little saving.

Approaching the seller's home, I couldn't help but marvel at how much Kilburn had changed. My first proper boyfriend had been from the area and, although he lived in a nice 'family home', this was also a time when the north-west – or North Wheezy, as it was often referred to – was becoming a magnet for gang activity. Even though you could tell that the homes had potential, the surrounding areas needed a lot of love. But on this day, it became apparent that the love had definitely pushed through. The road where the seller lived was lined with cherry blossoms. The loose, blush-coloured petals carpeted the tarmac like confetti from a big celebration balloon. And the celebration at hand?

Gentrification.

The areas I had known and loved even when they were a little rough around the edges all seemed to now be sprouting artisan cheese shops, and I noticed these shops had flyers in the window inviting you to mother and baby yoga. Of course, it was rare for me to ever need to cross the river, but when I did, I noticed this slow yet purposeful eviction of the people who had worked hard to make these communities vibrant and financially thriving. From hair shops to West Indian eateries, these local businesses were being shut down to make way for refurbished warehouses with dilapidated, 'distressed' decor, vegan pop-up venues and coffee houses packed full of Mac-laptop-touting white guys who wore expensive unbranded trainers, turned-up chinos and beanie hats that never seemed to fit their heads properly.

Oh, and they all rode 'fixed-wheel' bicycles. How anyone got anywhere on something with wheels that are fixed is beyond me. Gentrification and the way it destabilised those who had, in earlier times, made a great home out of a less than popular postcode, was rampant.

And this trip up to Kilburn reminded me that it was happening everywhere.

The front of the homes quite literally glowed with freshly Farrow-and-Ball-painted doors and highly coveted plantation shutters that sheltered the secret lives behind every other bay window. For the time of day, I was surprised to see the road so full of parked cars. The latest Range Rovers and BMWs sat less like automobiles and more like trophies. So much so that if you happened to be driving a car which wasn't polished well enough for you to do your lipstick using your reflection in its bonnet, then I would have suggested you park on a different road.

'I think we're almost there now,' I said to my sister.

She barely glanced up from her phone. I wanted to tell her off, but I was glad for the company. Again, I noted how strange it was to see how different our lives were now becoming. I should have expected it because I'm seven years older than her, but the pregnancy had put a mountain between us. She was still preoccupied with what to wear to the latest rave. And I assume she now took pity on me based on my lack of freedom, my waistline and depletion of any non-existent savings I had.

At last, we got to the house.

'Ehh ehh.' My sister looked up from her phone and laughed. 'They must have money, innit.'

The house was grand. We were greeted by a dark ivy door with stained glass accents allowing you a distorted peek through to the other side. I flicked the surprisingly heavy brass door knocker and allowed it to smack back onto the door, alerting the entire road to our arrival.

Through the stained glass, I could make out the pixellated image of a woman moving towards the door. Opening it ever so slightly, so much so that the gold door chain wasn't even strained, a blonde woman appeared. We could just about see a toddler balanced on her hip.

'I'm sorry,' she apologised, getting ready to close the door. 'I don't have time to sign up to any charity.'

'Err, I'm here for the pushchair?' I said, quickly checking my phone and glancing back at the number on the door to see if I was at the right address.

'Oh! Oh! I wasn't expecting . . . you so soon,' she said, fixing a smile onto her face but still not removing the chain from the lock.

My sister sighed. For fuck's sake, I thought to myself.

'Um, would you mind waiting here?' she asked.

And before I had even had the chance to respond, she turned and closed the door in our faces.

'Wow!' my sister said, so loudly she was borderline shouting.

'Girl, please, not now,' I said, shaking my head.

Before falling pregnant, I had been the confrontational one. Ready to rumble the minute I felt I had been disrespected or, even worse, judged too harshly. But whether it was the sickness of the first trimester or just the constant thought that acting raggo and raising my blood pressure no longer solely affected me, over the past few months I had mellowed out.

'Alright,' she agreed, clicking her tongue and rolling her eyes. We both knew what was happening here. But I was so close to getting my dream travel system, I wouldn't let these microaggressions spoil it now.

After what felt like forever, the woman returned with the pushchair, which was already fully erect. Taking her toddler off her hip and finally releasing the chain on the door, she began to push the chair towards us.

I couldn't help but break out into a smile.

'Do you have, um, a husband or boyfriend who can help you?' she asked, eyeing us up and down.

The blood-coloured top she wore really accentuated her cerulean eyes.

'He is at—' my sister began.

'He's waiting on the next street,' I said, hastily cutting her off mid-sentence. 'We went up and down this road and couldn't find a parking space anywhere.' I gave my sister the 'don't you dare speak' look.

'Yeah, he is waiting around the corner,' my sister snapped, pulling the chair away from the woman.

Suddenly, I caught myself.

'Oh, the money, forgive my manners.' I fumbled around in my handbag for the envelope I had stuffed full with notes. 'Two hundred and ten. It's all there. No need to count it.' I laughed nervously, knowing that she never would in front of me.

'Oh, err, thank you,' she said, taking the envelope away from me. She pointed at the pram. 'So, it's all there. Our rain cover had a hole in it, but you can pick one up cheaply anywhere.'

I had already anticipated this. The rain cover was going to be another twenty pounds. It would have to wait until Bode's next payday.

'No problem – got the most important thing now.' I smiled, backing away from her doorstep.

'Get home safe,' she said. 'Oh, and good luck with the baby.' She closed the door, a little more slowly than before. She might have warmed up, but I bet the moment my back was turned she whipped out a special pen to make sure the notes were real.

We had barely made it off her walkway before my sister let rip.

'I'm sorry, what was that? She wasn't expecting a black person, you know? And why did you lie to her? You should've told her that we were a lesbian couple. That would have pushed her over the edge. Here, give me that,' she demanded, snatching the handle of the buggy from me.

Yes, I thought. What was that?

I felt assaulted. From the immediate misconception that we were charity workers to how dismissive she was when she went to retrieve the pushchair, I knew the entire scenario was rooted in so much more than what happened at face value. In a mere seven-minute interaction, so many snap judgements had been made. It was clear that I didn't fit the profile of who she thought was coming to buy the pushchair. Was it my name that had fooled her? Or perhaps it was because my emails were void of any street slang? Whatever the reason, the shock on her face had been unmissable. Why the questions about my other half? Was it out of genuine concern about how we were getting the contraption home, or were we back in stereotype land? And why had I lied? So what if Bode wasn't there. Did that make a difference? No, of course not. I was overthinking it all, I told myself.

'Yeah, she clearly wasn't expecting a little black woman from South London,' I finally responded to my sister, not wanting to go down an emotional rabbit hole.

'Clearly,' my sister responded. 'Anyway, girl, you got the pushchair. Not gonna lie, it's cute, innit?' She smiled, tapping the invisible baby in the bassinet.

'Yes, it is,' I said, looking at the Bugaboo properly for the first time.

And at that moment, a moment so different from the ones shown in adverts or pictured in magazines, I think I felt a tiny stab of joy.

Against all odds, financial or otherwise, I had provided.

Like so many black mothers who had come before me, I was willing to go to the ends of the earth, or at the very least to north-west London, irrespective of circumstance. Yes, we didn't have much to hand right now. But I'd got this, and in getting this, I had to believe that we would get the chance to provide the baby with an abundance of everything further down the line.

Sure, it wasn't fresh out of a box, and it meant we would be living on tinned salmon and boxed rice for the next month. And it's funny how, now that this repetitive meal – which stirred up memories seasoned with longing – would help me get something I so dearly wanted, I wasn't so mad at it anymore. But, on that particularly fair-weathered day on a nondescript street in Kilburn, I felt like I had passed the first test – which was, no matter what was happening inside, make sure the world thinks you have your shit together. And with a travel system like this, I secretly hoped no one would dare doubt me or my baby.

4

ISO OMO LORUKO
(NAMING CEREMONY)

*'Job applications in British cities from people
with white-sounding names were 74% more likely
to receive a positive response than applications
from people with an ethnic minority name.'
(2009 research from NatCen Social Research,
commissioned by the government)*

What's in a name? Everything, apparently.

This issue was highlighted by David Cameron in his speech at the Conservative Party Conference in October 2015:

> [Name bias means] the disappointment of not get-
> ting your first choice of university place; it is being
> passed over for promotion and not knowing why;
> it's organisations that recruit in their own image and

aren't confident enough to do something different, like employing a disabled person or a young black man or woman.

Of course, I knew that. And as soon as I knew I was pregnant, one thing was as clear to me as almost anything: by the time my children's CVs reached a prospective employer, it was going to be beneficial to them that the interviewer would not know whether they were black. Because my name was Candice, it wasn't until I was invited to an interview that whoever was on the other side of the desk had any idea that I was black, and by then it was too late; they had no choice but to give me a chance to wow them. I knew absolutely that if my name had been, for example, LaQuisha, my chances of making it to that interview seat would have been less than likely.

Everybody who is black knows that. Living in a space where your proximity to whiteness usually determines your greatness is nothing new for us. We know that something as seemingly innocent as choosing a name for our child has to be carefully curated so it doesn't cause 'offence'. There's an element of fortune telling involved.

Now I was in the grip of the second trimester, insomnia had become my best friend. Stroking my growing and increasingly itchy belly, I spent the long nights scrolling through countless websites dedicated to the meanings of baby names. There would be no names like Avocado or Comet. My baby would have a name that meant business and was also racially ambiguous.

One morning, after another night of trawling, rejecting and drawing a blank, I had a brainwave. Sitting on the number 109 bus, gazing out of the window on the Streatham High Road, I had a name, a name that was asexual, just the right amount of cool and, to top it all off, paid homage to my hometown. Excitedly, I fumbled around the bottom of my handbag for my phone.

'What's the matter?' my mum said as soon as she answered. Since I had announced my pregnancy, every time I called anyone, it seemed as though they were expecting the worst.

'Mum, listen!' I said, smiling at the female passenger next to me. 'I think I've settled on the most perfect baby name.'

'Oh, thank God,' she said, her voice relaxing. 'It's taken you long enough.'

'Brixton!' I blurted out, startling my neighbour.

'What?' said Mum. 'You're in Brixton?'

'No!' I exclaimed. 'The name I've chosen is Brixton! It's Brixton!'

The line went suspiciously quiet. I felt my fellow passenger stop breathing in anticipation.

'Mum? Are you there?' I pulled the phone away from my ear to make sure the call was still connected. It was. I could hear a muffled, strained sound, almost like she was choking.

Unable to bear it any longer, she let out a huge laugh.

'Candice, what the hell?' she asked in between breaths. 'Brixton? No. No. No.'

I felt my eyes grow hot and heavy with tears. 'Mum, I have to go,' I said, and quickly snapped the phone shut.

I was furious. How dare she? Did she know how long I had agonised over this? In those few moments between making the decision and calling her, I had already decided that I was going to call the baby Brix for short. I loved how punchy it was.

Unfortunately, Bode was just as unimpressed as my mother.

'You what?' he asked.

'BRIX-TON,' I enunciated. 'You know, like the place.' I fixed my face so he could see I was deadly serious.

'I understand perfectly what you mean,' he said, his words unravelling slowly as if I were hot soil and he was unsure whether there was a landmine hiding below the surface.

I tightened my features even further.

'Yeah, I don't think that's going to work,' he continued, carefully. His hands were together under his chin, as if he were about to pray.

I swallowed hard.

'What's wrong with it?' I snapped.

He raised his hands as if trying to prove to the police he was weaponless.

'Listen, I just think it's a little, well, ghetto,' he replied, whispering the last word as if the walls could hear and would take offence. I tucked my chin into my chest and let my eyes narrow into slits. Although the term 'ghetto' has now since been co-opted, reworked, repackaged and resold to us by way of gold hoop name-plate earrings and the Kardashian cane-rows (I jest), when a black person references the ghetto it's almost always something that we are trying to get away from, not something that we should have to pay to be a part of.

'Ghetto? Really?' I was livid, my voice hard and rising. 'And who decides what that is?'

'The world, unfortunately.' Bode shrugged.

'My child will be called Brixton and that is the end of it,' I shouted, before trying and failing to run up the stairs. 'I'm the one having the sleepless nights and heartburn! Not you! And I will call my child whatever I like!'

Looking back now on this moment of madness, I can't help but laugh. Who did I think I was? Gwyneth Paltrow? I didn't have the correct skin tone nor the buoyant bank balance to support this hormone-fuelled choice. And whether I wanted to admit it or not, Bode had a point. Even though Brixton is now home to oyster bars and flat whites priced at seven pounds a cup, at that time the only things that would have come to people's minds were KFC, Speedy Noodle (RIP), a handful of hair shops and the imposing Somerleyton estate. On reflection, maybe a name that was synonymous with weaves and riots was perhaps not the best one to give my child.

The truth was, I knew why the naming of my child was

so fraught. One of my most enduring memories is when my father sat me down to watch *Roots*. I must have been no older than eight. These days, I have no idea what my dad was thinking. He did offer up some light-hearted trigger warning that I may perhaps find the movie 'a little disturbing', but, he assured me, it was important to watch as much as possible because it was part of our history.

Wide-eyed and traumatised, I watched people who looked very similar to me being treated no better than dogs. Actually, I thought, dogs were usually fed and stroked on the head. So no, this was worse.

A scene that has stuck with me until this very day is when Kunta Kinte, a Gambian man who had been taken by force from his village and sold as a slave to a plantation owner in Virginia in the USA, is being whipped because he won't agree to his slave master's name change.

Panting and afraid, arms tied aloft with his dense black body swaying to and fro from each swing of the whip, he stands firm in declaring his name is Kunta, whilst his 'master' shouts at him to take the name 'Toby'. The whipping continues until, exhausted and near death, Kunta finally relents.

The slave master makes him say it loud and clear, before calling him a good nigger.

Not long after that scene, I ran out of my dad's house in tears.

He didn't immediately come after me. Perhaps there was a lesson in having to sit with the pain. Like the characters I had just watched being tortured. When he did come out of the house to find me, he pulled me into his chest. 'I'm sorry, Cand,' he whispered.

And, despite the comfort of his arms, I stood there sobbing for God knows how long.

That was my first indelible lesson in understanding that the names we black people carried weren't actually our own. Although I was young, I understood enough to know that people like Kunta Kinte and I were in some way or another inextricably linked. Long before tracing DNA or ancestry became something that was central to primetime BBC and advertised by Instagram influencers, I knew that I was Kunta Kinte and he was me, and my name, more specifically my last name, couldn't possibly have started out as Brown or Brathwaite.

I didn't need any DNA or provenance hunters to understand that ever since my ancestors were taken from their rightful birthplace – the land they had governed and owned – they were taught, first by force and then by trend, to assimilate. To hide in plain sight. To pull themselves in so tight to the proximity of whiteness, because it would be this and only this that saved their lives. As the decades pressed on, it was a trend that endured all the way into the twenty-first century, when the easier your name is to pronounce – or better yet, if it's a name that can be betrothed to the white race – the greater your chance of succeeding will be.

'I named you after one of my favourite actresses,' Dad

said with a smile when I asked him for clarification of my own name later that summer.

I wasn't yet confident enough to have an explicit conversation about what I'd seen in Kunta's renaming. So, like a child who'd been warned not to eat the entire cake, I was simply picking at the edges.

'Why?' he asked. 'Don't you like it?'

I hadn't much thought about it. I had met no one with my name, so that was cool. But there was something I didn't like about my surname, and that was its length. It was double-barrelled – Brown-Brathwaite – and it never fit on one line on the front of any of my schoolbooks.

'It's OK, I guess.'

'It's more than OK,' he said. 'I have it on good word that in Ethiopia, your name means "queen".' He winked, softly pinching the back of my neck in a way only he could.

'Really?' I said, my chest visibly inflating.

'Yup.' He laughed. 'Not so nonchalant now, are we?'

Now, as an adult, I'm even more in love with my first name. It's that perfect balance of being racially ambiguous, allowing me to gain access to rooms before anyone knows what I look like, whilst its actual meaning, although perhaps only known to me (and now you), is overwhelmingly black.

But when it came to choosing the name for my own baby, I really struggled to replicate that; even more so because no matter how we diced it, even if we found a first name that could slip through the net of the most racially biased job recruiter, they were going to have a Nigerian last name. Bode's last name was Aboderin.

And there was definitely no masking that.

With this in the back of my mind, and the strained and strange duality of trying to make their lives easier by providing my children with their version of 'Toby' whilst also trying to remind them that, deep down, they will always be 'Kunta', there were some names I filed immediately under the 'no' column.

Any name that referenced a car was out. So, Bentley, Lexus, Mercedes, Audi or any other vehicle brand were definite no-nos. Then, names such as Shanay-nay, Devonté, LaToya or any other name that could be associated with an American sitcom or novel were also out. I'll tell you for free that Beyoncé only gets away with her name because she became Beyoncé, the mega-diva popstar. Five-year-olds that have been named in her honour aren't going to get an easy time of it. I also wanted to steer clear of names that were actual words, such as Ebony, Diamond, Star, Prince and Deja (add the Vu if you're feeling adventurous).

Also, there would be no fucking fruity names either. We weren't rich enough to get away with names like Apple, Peaches or Mango. I would have to leave that to celebrities. Also, no names of colours or drinks were permitted.

If it were to be a boy, I was vehemently against giving him a 'heavy' name. For example, there are only two men who come to mind when I think of Martin or Malcolm, and I didn't want to weigh down any son straight out of the womb with that kind of expectation. The world would have enough time to do that. I also knew that there were certain names you just knew had to be that of a black man: Hakeem, Kwanza, Malachi, Pharaoh, King, Wendell, Otis, Treyvon, LaBron and Xavier all conjured up images of strong and beautiful black men – and that was the opposite of what I was trying to achieve. My baby would no doubt be strong and beautiful, but I didn't want anyone to know that he was black until he had the chance to prove himself. And for anyone who's wondering if I'm perhaps overthinking it, I'll put it on my life that that is your privilege talking. Only those of us who have to birth children in a space that isn't designed to support them would lose sleep over something which seems as trivial as a name.

'I think you should go with something biblical,' my mum offered up one afternoon after listening to Bode and I go around in metaphorical circles for an hour.

'Mum.' I sighed, trying not to roll my eyes. 'How many times do I have to tell you that I'm not really into those Bible names?'

'And that's the problem!' she said. 'You want to put some protection on the child's head! A biblical name would make them go far.'

I knew now was not the time to remind her that it was my child and I would name them whatever I wanted, and it certainly wasn't going to be Abel, Mary, Gideon, Ruth,

Solomon, Esther or Zechariah. And plus, she was one to talk. Her name was June and her brother, my uncle, was called Philip. My dad was called Richard and his brother was called Anthony. It was clear that similar thinking to mine had gone into what was going onto their birth certificates.

It felt as if Bode was reading my mind.

'Honestly, if it's a boy I think we should just call him Richard, after your dad,' he added, his voice softening, to indicate he knew how much I wished my dad was here to see his grandchild.

I pursed my lips.

It's not that I didn't like the name Richard. I did. I liked even more the fact that it did what I needed a name to do, which was to move in plain sight. But what I didn't like was the idea that he might grow up thinking that he had to live up to the namesake of a man he had never met. I could imagine him growing up and not being best pleased with us.

Also, despite Bode's thoughtfulness, it still pained me that I was about to become a mother and my beloved father wasn't around. I didn't want to have to explain how tender it felt to have to think about him at this time.

'And what if it's a girl?' I shot back, hoping to end that part of the conversation there.

'I really like Esmé,' Bode said.

And as he said it, something within me moved and I couldn't be sure it wasn't the baby or butterflies.

'Oh, that's nice!' exclaimed Mum. 'It could be Esmé for short, but it could be Esmeralda.'

'No!' Bode and I laughed, in unison.

'But I'm not mad on Esmé,' I said, looking up to the ceiling as if it would provide me with clarity. 'Although I feel like I've heard it before.'

On cue, Bode began to hum a song both of us knew so well. And I couldn't help but smile. That was it! It was the name of Edward's mum in the *Twilight* series: Esme Cullen. We'd bonded over our love of the vampire fantasy early on in our relationship.

Something moved within me again. Yeah, I liked that name! It was racially ambiguous, beautiful and, I later found out, had a sweet meaning – to be loved. And a bit like the baby itself, over time the name grew on me.

The next important thing for me was that it was imperative the middle name was Nigerian – Yoruba, to be precise. It was a way to honour the tribe Bode was from. I knew the time would come when my child would want to explore that side of their heritage, and I wanted her or him to know, or to at the very least feel – if I happened to not be around for them – that I had encouraged them to do so.

It was only then I learned that there was a ritual in the Nigerian community called the 'naming ceremony', more commonly known to Yorubas, as Iso Omo Loruko, which usually happens eight days after the baby's birth.

'Eight days?!' I squealed at Bode. 'I've never done this

before, but I'm pretty sure my vagina will still resemble an inside-out kebab! There is no way that is happening.'

As with all things pertaining to his culture which I childishly wrote off, he just laughed.

'Listen, I'm only letting you know what would happen if we were back home. You're British. My parents don't expect that of you.' He flicked his wrist, as if to do away with the matter.

I didn't tell him at the time, but that hurt. And the sting was pronounced because it was peppered with truth. As a black British woman of Caribbean descent, it was only now that I was about to have a child that I noticed that there was a lot about my culture and my heritage – outside of putting too much vinegar on my chips, my love for Ribena and my weakness for plantain – that I did not know. All of a sudden I felt like a child myself, trying to grab at anything which I could possibly pass down to my child as a rite of passage. This was definitely something I would have to work on resolving later.

Finally, the last piece in the name puzzle was the surname. When it came to figuring out last names – or, more precisely, the order of them – that was a whole new level of intense consideration. Brathwaite is my maiden name and I'm very protective of it for reasons which perhaps began before I even knew my own name at all.

'It was when I was actually in labour with you,' Mum would always begin, before her retelling of the infamous family drama that went down hours before I was born. 'Your dad's parents were not happy with the fact that I decided to give you a double-barrelled surname. They came into the labour ward, shouting and screaming about how you should have only your father's name, Brown. But I wasn't having any of it; I wanted my name, Brathwaite, in there too. The argument was so explosive it raised my blood pressure immediately and you were born via emergency C-section shortly after.'

'The way I see it is,' she continued, her long dreadlocks framing her slim face and making her almond eyes even more pronounced, 'no one but me understands the pain it took to bring you here. I wasn't just going to hand over the right of naming you to your father and his family. The only way your birth certificate was going to read Brown was if it read Brathwaite too. Anything could happen, and look, it did.'

It did indeed. Firstly, my parents broke up when I was eight months old, due to my father's philandering becoming public knowledge. He was upset. Now, whether he was upset because he caused my mother pain and embarrassment or because he had been found out, we may never know, but he hastily tried to fix his mess and asked for her hand in marriage. She rightly refused. And the reason I know this scenario to be factual is because I'm in possession of the handwritten love letters he sent to her from Jamaica, where he ran off to 'clear his head' when she decided to call it quits.

His undeniable angle-filled scrawl illustrated his pain, but for my mother, there was no going back.

For years I bore his name along with hers, but after his death, his parents and widow wanted no more to do with me, the sole carrier of his name. At his funeral, they made it clear that they found my mere presence to be a terrible inconvenience. Standing outside his home (I wasn't allowed in) watching floral arrangements arrive, I felt my young blood begin to boil with anger. The wreaths read 'SON', 'BROTHER' and 'HUSBAND'. No one had taken it upon themselves to remember that he was a father. By the time I had made it to the church by cab, there was a distinct heaviness in the air. Glancing down at the service sheet, I saw something else that was like a punch in the stomach: I had been left off the order of service. This was not the mistake of a grieving family, but instead the masterful planning of adults who didn't want to acknowledge that their meal ticket had a child after all. After being embarrassed beyond description, I left knowing there was one thing I could do to make myself feel better, and that was to drop the name Brown with immediate effect. From that very day I've been known solely as Brathwaite, and I've never been more thankful for my mother's foresight.

And now, years later, Bode and I were having the same argument; it had just changed slightly. Bode understood my requirement for a double-barrelled name, as it would mean that if we were to have a daughter, she would be at liberty to pick a name for the situation. But what we couldn't seem to agree on is which name came last. General tradition dictated that, in the case of double-barrelled surnames, the man's family name should come last. And Bode was in strong agreement.

'Nope. I absolutely do not agree to Brathwaite being last. No. No. Hell fucking no!' Bode shouted from the hallway as I folded baby clothes in what would become the nursery.

I rolled my eyes and clicked my tongue. 'I don't understand what the problem is,' I shouted back, repositioning my legs to give my ever-growing stomach more room.

'I'll be frank, Candice,' Bode answered, entering the room. 'Here's what the problem is. You move like you're a single parent or like you're waiting for me to fuck you over at any minute. Why does your name have to be last? Do you know how gracious I'm being by agreeing to this double-barrel bullshit? Because that's what it is, it's bullshit. Look, I'm really sorry that your dad fucked your mum over and she had to raise you single-handedly, but stop trying to relive a negative past. Give us the space to at least try to make this work.'

I sat there, stunned and silenced, both things a rarity for me.

And it was rare to see him so . . . passionate. Yes. There was an air of being pissed off, but there was definitely more passion than anything else. His words sliced through me like the sharpest of paper cuts, and the sting penetrated parts of me which I didn't even know were there.

Was I worried about being left alone to raise this baby?

Constantly.

The odds just didn't seem favourable. I was surrounded by women whose long-term relationships were with their kids and not the men who got them pregnant. Whilst I wasn't saying it out loud, could my subconscious think that trying to have control of a name was a way to help mentally prepare myself for what I believed was the inevitable, a future that consisted of me constantly on the phone to the Child Support Agency because my child's father wouldn't stand up to his responsibilities? A future of being a baby mother?

Perhaps.

Maybe.

Who knew?

But what I did know was that in that moment, I had alarming clarity. I heard Bode's words and I understood that in order to make a change, perhaps we were going to have to do something differently. Everything within me told me to take the leap.

'Fine.' I shrugged, not wanting to let on how much his words had simultaneously cut me open and opened me up.

'Sorry, what?' he asked.

'I said fine,' I repeated, unwilling to shake my sassy demeanour off. 'You heard me.'

He paused, cocking his head to one side, clearly trying to assess me, but I wouldn't let my gaze meet his. He crouched down in front of me.

'Candice. Whilst I have no doubt that you've let me in

here,' he said, poking my chest roundabout where my heart was, 'I often wonder what it will take for you to let me in here.'

He gently pressed his forefinger onto my temple. I swatted at his hand like I would a fly. Sighing, he rose to his feet and left me with my thoughts and the laundry.

Later, as I spoke to my mum and told her what we'd decided, I sighed as she told me I was making 'a huge mistake'.

'Your name should come last, always,' she told me. 'Who knows what will happen?'

'Do you know what, Mum,' I said, sure about not being sure for the first time in all this naming business. 'Nobody knows. But if one thing is certain, it won't be a repeat of when I was born because I'm already here. I'm not saying Bode is perfect, but for the love of God, could we not go into every situation expecting the worst?'

I couldn't believe that this much thought had to go into a name. I felt like there was a sincere struggle between trying to be ahead of the game and think about how the world would perceive our children, and also not being a victim. And whilst there were far more abrasive things to be, none had the same effect on me as being a victim. Why couldn't I just name my kid whatever the fuck I wanted? Did it have to be so complicated?

I now knew the answers.

No, I couldn't.

And yes, it did.

5

BLACK GIRLS DON'T CRY

Black British women are five times more likely
to die in childbirth compared to white women.
(2018 MBRRACE-UK)

'Black babies have a 121% increased risk of
being stillborn and a 50% increased risk of
neonatal death (i.e. dying within 28 days
after birth) compared to white babies.'
(Government response to a petition put forward
to Parliament on 22nd October 2019)

'Well, I've got plenty of old towels here if that's the route you've decided to go down.' Mum sighed.

It was. I was resolute in my plan to have a home birth, and now the time was swiftly approaching, I was trying to finalise the last few things I would need.

This wasn't exactly going down well.

'I just don't understand why you wouldn't want to be in a space where medical professionals would be immediately available,' Bode pressed when I showed him a picture of the birth pool we would need.

'Because birth is not supposed to be a medical experience,' I replied.

I knew that the cost of a home birth worried him. The hiring of the birth pool alone was going to set us back a few hundred quid. But I had made up my mind.

'Furthermore,' I went on, 'the idea of medical intervention scares the crap out of me.'

I wasn't lying; I hadn't ever even broken a bone, let alone pushed a watermelon out of my vagina. And I was scared. Nine months is a long time to digest information which could make a first-time mother fearful. I was no different. I'd spent a pretty penny on trying to get hold of the literary material that spoke to me about giving birth, and even that had been a painful task in itself.

I had struggled through so many books and articles which talked about labour and motherhood in such broad, non-racially-specific terms that I found myself seeking out Stateside material by African-American women, as that seemed to be all that was available when it came to black women's experiences of giving birth. It was important to me because my mother had suffered from pre-eclampsia and from what I had read, black women seemed to be more at risk of pregnancy-related illness. And whilst some of the personal stories in these books were relevant to being black and pregnant, overall, because the US healthcare system is so different to ours, the language in which these books were written didn't really explain what I was going to face.

So, I had no choice but to turn to books by Ina May Gaskin, the original home-birth evangelist, with titles like *The Guide to Childbirth* and *Spiritual Midwifery*. And although her books were completely void of any description of pregnancy or birth for black women, I took heart from the images and words that depicted birth as an almost-spiritual experience. Because, whilst we now live in an era in which medical intervention is possible, I knew that my ancestors had seen birth as more of a natural process that would unfold in its own time rather than a medical emergency. And I was scared to death by the idea of a C-section, which is why I wasn't best pleased when it was mentioned at my thirty-eight-week appointment.

I had walked the almost two miles to the hospital at quite a quick rate considering how far along I was. Throughout the entire pregnancy, I had made it my duty to be as healthy as possible. Because of my concerns surrounding pre-eclampsia, anything I could do to make sure that I didn't become a statistic, I did.

I was almost winded by the time I reached the clinic, but was proud that I was still able to walk at least twenty miles a week. Approaching the waiting room of the maternity area, I gave my name and DOB to the receptionist and waddled along to the seating area.

I despised these appointments. I had three different mid-wives: a petite, hijab-wearing woman, who had no kids; a tall, middle-aged black woman, who had two children; and an equally as tall white woman, who had one child.

If my maternity care had been a bid for diversity and inclusion, it would have been hitting it out of the park. But it wasn't, because even though all three women were so different, I found their lack of availability and inability to listen strikingly similar. And so, admittedly, I became relaxed about attending some appointments. I made sure to monitor my own blood pressure and to count the kicks, because that's all they ever seemed to do at these sessions. When someone at the clinic did finally notice that no one had seen me in six weeks, I would be summoned and I'd obediently go, but I'd always want the appointments to be over as quickly as they began.

But today was different. I was approaching the last stretch and I was eager to know what was going on down there.

At thirty-eight weeks, I was well and truly over being pregnant. By now we had found out we were having a girl, and she was definitely going to be called Esmé. I had really wanted a boy, and secretly I think Bode did too, although our reasons for this were very different. I was fearful of raising a girl, especially considering how tumultuous my own relationship with my mother was. For Bode it was far simpler; he was already a father to an almost-seven-year-old girl, and I think he wanted a son just because it would have made for a different experience. But, as the months went on, we couldn't help but imagine her little face. The weight of Esmé's tiny body felt like carrying a bowling ball. Also – although all the material I had read assured me that the baby's movements would soon lessen due to lack of space – this kid seemed to be hell-bent on breaking my ribs. Any woman who has been pregnant will know that sleeping is hard enough, but at almost nine months pregnant I was often reduced to tears by my baby, who clearly had a fondness for breakdancing.

'Candice?'

Slowly, I got to my feet and looked for a face to match the voice.

I was greeted by the most beautiful sight: a black woman, as short as me. Trying to do the maths on a black woman's age is always hard. I wanted to put her in the late fifties, but, because black really doesn't crack, she could've been nearer to seventy. Her close-cropped Caesar haircut was the same as mine, except it was peppered with silver. Her face was covered with moles, her eyes were dark but loving, and her smile was inviting. It was like looking at my own future.

'Come in, my dear, come, come. Take a seat.' She guided me into her consulting room and tapped the chair closest to her desk.

It took a while for me to place the melodies in her accent, but finally I clocked that she was Guyanese.

'I'm sorry about the wait,' she began, flipping through my notes.

She went on to say that she had been a midwife for over thirty years, and she confirmed she was originally from Guyana. She asked me how I was feeling and never once glanced at the clock when I explained that I was finding the continuous movements of the baby extremely painful.

'And you are . . . almost thirty-nine weeks,' she said, running her finger down some paperwork. 'No, you shouldn't be feeling that way at all. That baby should be settling and getting ready for the madness of the world. Let's do all the usual bits and bobs. And after that, I'll do my own observations.'

As per usual, everything was fine. Luckily, although pre-eclampsia is usually hereditary, I seemed to have escaped its swollen grasp.

'Hop up on here,' she said, then she laughed, catching herself. 'Of course, I don't mean hop, just get up here as best as you can.'

I laughed too. I felt relaxed and at ease, a rarity during these appointments.

Out of nowhere, a bit like Mary Poppins, she pulled a measuring tape out of thin air. Measuring all around my swollen midsection, she ummed and ahhed to herself. Gently she ran her finger down the now blackened linea nigra, which was even more pronounced due to the abundance of melanin in my skin. As she approached the base of the line, she again measured with her fingers. Then she went on to scoop her hands underneath the bump and search around for the baby's head. Her facial expression dithered between confusion and concern before finally settling on wonder.

'You sure you're thirty-eight weeks?' she asked.

I nodded.

'Well, I hate to tell you, but this baby's head isn't even engaged. I've done this job a long time and this child isn't coming out alone. The child's comfort, combined with your frame, I think it's a guaranteed C-section.'

All of a sudden, she was the ugliest woman I had ever met.

'No!' I cried out. 'No! I've got everything ready for a home birth.'

'I'm sorry, Candice,' she said. 'I know it is not nice and it will come as a shock, but I have to be honest. What annoys me the most is that, because it's your first child, they are gonna do all manner of foolishness when really they should just schedule a section, because we all know how this will end.'

I wasn't listening. I was already sitting upright, getting the god-awful gel they use to listen to the baby's heartbeat off of my stomach. I had sat up too fast and now my head was spinning, but I wanted to get out of the office as fast as I could. Like most black elders, she was unmoved by my obvious impatience.

'Other than that, the baby is in good health,' she said, turning to me. 'Just going to need a little help to evict it,' she added with a little laugh.

I swallowed my tears, grabbed back my NHS maternity

book, which contained all my patient notes, and left without saying goodbye.

I called Bode. He always insisted on an immediate update after any appointment he couldn't attend. He kissed his teeth. 'Babe, don't cry, please. You know I hate it when you cry. Listen, no matter what happens, we will get through it together.'

Of course, I thought, murderously. He would find a way to silently agree with her. He had always been heavily against the idea of home birth.

As it turned out, a home birth was not to be. And just as the Guyanese midwife predicted, my little baby politely ignored the eviction notice. At almost two weeks overdue, I was in hospital to induce labour. After three sweeps, two nights sleeping in a labour ward and the insertion of a pessary, we were all hoping I would soon begin the process of labour myself.

Already, it hadn't been the nicest experience. Bode had routinely picked up on sighs and eye-rolls from every question he asked. The night before had ended in cross words when I'd hastily been given painkillers and he'd challenged the midwife as to what they were.

I'd had it up to here with the midwives, but I was doing my best to remain pleasant and compliant. I'd spoken to plenty of friends who had warned me to stay on the best side of the maternity staff, as they'd all noticed that when they'd complained or made a 'fuss', the very little care they had been receiving immediately went out of the staffroom window.

Morning three of my stay and I was still only one centimetre dilated. Bode wanted to go home for a shower, which seemed fair enough, but I hated it when he left me alone on the ward.

'You gonna get a cab?' I asked.

He shook his head.

'Nah, I'll walk.'

It broke my heart, really. We'd agreed that the little bit of cash we'd been able to save would be better spent when the baby was earthside. So, in the middle of what felt like the coldest winter ever, Bode had been doing the two-mile walk between our home and the hospital on foot.

After he left, I felt I was in the scariest place I could be, which was alone with my thoughts. But before I had time to allow myself to panic too much, a young midwife and a doctor appeared.

'Right . . . Candice? Yes, Candice,' the doctor confirmed to himself, making more eye contact with his clipboard than with me.

I struggled to sit up.

'We've come to take you to a labour suite, where I will proceed to break your waters,' he said.

'I'm sorry, what?'

'Break. Your. Waters,' he repeated, pausing between each word as if he were talking to an insubordinate toddler.

'Oh. I heard. You,' I snapped, kissing my teeth. 'But what I need you to explain is what that process is and why you've waited for my partner to leave to come and tell me this.'

Finally, he made full eye contact with me. He was very tall, and the tone of his skin reminded me of the men I'd seen whilst travelling in India. His hair was jet-black and stiff with some kind of pomade. His matching moustache was far too overgrown, so it seemed as if he only had one lip, a protruding bottom one which made his facial expression seem permanently soured. I set my facial expression to match his lack of enthusiasm.

'Right. So, we've tried all we can thus far to get your baby out and it—'

'She,' I corrected him.

'She.' He sighed. 'She seems to be resisting. The next step is for me to medically break your waters using a slim needle with a hook attached to the end. Hopefully doing so will send a signal to it – her – and we can perhaps get this show on the road. To help speed things up, we will also put you on a hormone drip.'

I felt the world slip out from beneath me. With every step, we seemed to be edging closer and closer towards the birth I didn't want. I'd watched a documentary about this. It was called *The Business of Being Born* and was presented by Ricki Lake. Despite being comforted by the fact I recognised Ricki's face due to Nan's TV habits decades before, I was left traumatised by the findings of the documentary, which, although it was focused on the US, gave great insight into how birth was no longer seen as a natural process that needed time to unravel, but instead a race against the clock to get as many women from bed to baby and beyond as quickly as possible. To help speed things up was the use of synthetic hormones, designed to trick the woman's body and therefore the baby into believing it was in labour. If it had helped women deliver naturally, maybe I would have found it easier to digest, but according to the evidence, over ninety per cent of births that faced intervention by way of hormone drip resulted in a C-section.

Until now there had always been the option of going home and trying to wait things out, but at this point, I doubted they would let me leave. So, after what felt like hours but, in reality, was most probably seconds, I nodded my head in agreement, as long as they gave me time to text Bode first.

Within seconds my phone vibrated: 'WTF?! I AM COMING NOW. MAKE THEM WAIT!'

The doctor appeared again, this time with some sort of chariot. Shuffling off the bed, I lowered myself into the wheel-chair with one bag filled with my personal belongings and another full of things for the baby precariously balanced on what little room was left on my lap. He weaved me around the ward until we arrived at what to most would have seemed like a very large, inviting birthing suite full of reassuring midwives. Me? I saw it as a prison. I knew good and well that once that hormone drip kicked in, they wouldn't even allow me to walk the parameters of the space. I would be strapped to the bed until it was time to deliver the baby.

'Right,' said the doctor, helping me onto the bed. 'If you could open your legs as wide as you can, please.'

I lifted my head off the flimsy pillow just in time to see him coming towards me with what can only be described as a knitting needle on steroids. Silver in colour, on one end – the end that was spearheading its way to my muff – there was a distinct loop-like feature very much like Captain Hook's hand replacement.

'Woah, woah, where the fuck do you think you're putting that?' I yelled, as he put his face quite literally into my vagina. I snapped my knees shut.

'Ma'am, this is the tool we use to break your waters. I promise you won't feel any discomfort. Just some slight pressure,' he said, briefly emerging.

'Slight pressure?! Bloody well looks like you're trying to drag my heart out of me, but anyway, as you were,' I allowed him, slowly letting my legs fall open.

He disappeared again underneath my gown. Just when I thought he didn't know what he was doing, I felt an almighty sense of relief and a gush I couldn't control. In a swift moment he appeared before me again, but this time, his scrubs were a little damp. Both my waters and the tension between us were broken. We both laughed and with that more water came out.

'So, is this how it's gonna be, then?' I said. 'Am I just going to wet myself until she makes an entrance?'

'Well, unfortunately, yes,' he replied. 'If her head was engaged, you wouldn't be losing so much water. Hopefully this will get her to hurry, and the more she comes down, the less water you will lose.'

But it made no difference. An hour or so later, they hooked me up to the drip.

The room was buzzing with professionals. In and out they would sweep, checking vital signs and talking to everyone except me, the patient. There was one woman whose energy I did appreciate. She was a kind-eyed, soft-spoken black mid-wife. Who at every step in the process tried to reassure me that I was up to the task. She would intermittently stroke my shoulder or talk me through a contraction. It felt like time was flying by and soon the room was populated with familiar faces. Bode had returned and now my mum, sister and nan had all gathered. The first grandchild, the first niece and the first great-grandchild – they weren't going to miss a moment of her arrival. The energy in the room swayed between anxious and excited.

And as my kind-eyed black midwife warned me, the contractions ranged between soft cramps to what I can only imagine is how it feels when a great white shark chews down on your abdomen.

I will spare you any further details, as this is not my auto-biography, but I can tell you it was all a hideous nightmare and I ended up in surgery and Esmé was born by Caesarean. The Guyanese midwife I had seen previously had been right.

But I was by then way too tired and fed up to care anymore. The main thing was to get her out safely.

As soon as Esmé was brought forth, she was whisked away to be weighed and checked for distress. I couldn't see or touch my baby. I had to lay there whilst they sewed me shut and I tried to get blurred glimpses of her.

'Is she OK?' I croaked.

'Yes! Yes! She is perfect,' Bode responded.

And that was enough for me.

Once I was out of the theatre, I was wheeled to a recovery room it seemed my nan had argued her way into. My eyesight was still blurry as I had not yet been given my glasses back, but from the corner of my eye I could make out a plastic cot, which, by my nan's reaction, I assumed had my baby in it.

'Oh, she is divine!' Nan cooed.

'She's beautiful,' said the lovely midwife who had been with me in the theatre. 'What's her name?'

'Esmé-Olivia,' I whispered.

'Esmé-Olivia,' she repeated, looking into the hospital cot with a look of wonder, which I'm almost sure was solely reserved for these tender moments. I've heard midwives say that they could see a baby be born a thousand times, but still every birth felt brand new and wondrous. That was the complete opposite to how I was feeling. I felt old and beat up. I was trying to find the joy in this moment, but I was flat-out exhausted. She then told me that she would have to go and tend to another mother-to-be, but that if she could, she would be back before I was discharged the next day. I thanked her and then she was gone.

Whilst my nan and sister fussed over Esmé, a new midwife arrived. A short black woman, she seemed unperturbed by the joy of new life and could barely muster a smile, unlike the midwife before her.

'Time to get this baby on the breast,' she ordered, scooping Esmé up like you would a bag of carrots from your local supermarket. Without asking, she opened my robe.

'What are you doing?!' I said, taken aback.

'Well, we can't feed her through the robe, can we?' she said, crossly.

I kissed my teeth.

Without saying a word, Nan stepped in. The midwife had the sense to step back. Ever so gently, my nan tried to encourage Esmé to latch onto my breast.

'OK.' Nan laughed as I let out a soft shriek. 'She's got it.'

So, in the end I had my beautiful baby girl, but it hadn't been the best experience. However, there was way worse to come once I left the hospital . . .

Around day three of being home, I realised something was wrong. I'd been complaining to all three of the midwives who'd been sent to my home to take stock of my recovery. I seemed to be feeling worse rather than better. Every night I would sweat through to the mattress, but I was told by each one of them that it was just my hormones trying to recalibrate themselves and my body getting rid of water weight.

My dizzy and overall fuzzy light-headedness was put down to lack of sleep. And when I pulled my trousers down to show them a raised lump gathering beneath the C-section wound, I was told that was more than likely just some scar tissue starting to form.

Truth be told, I felt horrid and I knew there was something far more sinister at play, but no medical professional was listening. Bode did his best to adjust to being responsible for the entire household. By this time, I had given up on trying to breastfeed Esmé and I couldn't even take the stairs, so Bode had to get anything the baby or I needed. He was exhausted too, and although I don't think he doubted what I was saying, I do think he was too tired to register how serious my discomfort could potentially be. The only one who kept pushing me to head back to the hospital was my nan. Maybe she was in maternal mode and just wanted me to be checked out, or maybe it was due to another dream, but either way she encouraged me to keep speaking up for myself. However, after being told it was all normal, even I began to doubt myself. Did I truly feel as bad as I did or was this all in my head? If those who had studied medicine with the hopes of making people feel better were treating me as if nothing was wrong, who was I to argue?

It was the horrific smell that awoke me. The scent was so bad, it was like the Hulk had taken a shit and forgotten to flush. I'd fallen asleep whilst trying to soothe Esmé, and she had paid me back by dropping a poonami so rank it awoke the entire household.

'Jesus Christ!' Bode exclaimed as he stumbled into the bedroom, rubbing the sleep from his eye. 'Here, let me change her.'

I knew that was his way of sliding me an olive branch. When she had awoken for the fifth time that night, the tired and strained energy between us had exploded and we had had a blazing row. I had stormed off (admittedly, it was more of a shuffle!) with her into the spare room, where we had both finally fallen asleep.

Whilst Bode was seeing to Esmé, I felt something wet and slimy oozing down my legs. I opened the drawstring on Bode's tracksuit bottoms that I had taken to wearing since I came home.

I screamed his name.

Later on, when we would recount what happened to each other, Bode would describe the feeling of his belly falling to his feet when he clocked that Esmé's nappy was empty. And I would describe a feeling of victory. Victory because I now had proof that something was going wrong. Now I smelt like a rotting pig, they would definitely have to believe me.

The stuff oozing out of me was green and black. The scent was so violent I had to run to the kitchen to throw up. Bode called an ambulance and then my nan. By the time the blue lights of the ambulance lit up the entire road, my nan's trusty Ford Fiesta came to a screeching halt. She looked panicked, but upon seeing my face she quickly put her guard up, instructing Bode to call my mum and stay with Esmé.

'Right, Candice,' one of the kind paramedics was saying. 'We're going to get you to the hospital straight away.'

I can't quite remember the ambulance ride. I felt like I was already outside of my body watching the entire scene unfold. Sometimes I answered the questions the paramedic asked and sometimes I didn't. By the time we arrived at the hospital, I was barely conscious.

Once they had me in a private bay, a doctor quickly came to assess me. The smell alone spoke a thousand words. I could see that some of the nurses were visibly repulsed and I overheard a few other patients complaining.

Soon I was transferred back to the labour ward. The sound of screaming babies made my breasts hurt. I was horrendously engorged. Esmé was formula fed, so this meant that unless I expressed, my milk had nowhere to go but back up and make my tits harder than Dolly Parton's.

When the doctor came back to see me, she told me that I was slipping into septic shock and that they were preparing the theatre. The weight of Esmé's baby body caused a pus-filled sack above my C-section wound to burst, the contents of which had already started to infect my bloodstream. I started crying so hard I started to shake. Everybody was panicky, scared and worried. I had the operation and, after I came round, I was once again in a private room surrounded by my entire family. I later found out that they had taken the whole medical team to task as to why no one had listened to me.

Days turned into weeks. When a stern Nigerian doctor

and four students came to remove the tubes from me, I recognised one of them as an ex-classmate of mine. She worked hard to avoid my gaze, but then considering the only thing left to look at was my vagina, we were both in an awkward position. The joy.

The doctor was rough, and when she tugged the tubes from my sides, it felt as if a snake were trying to escape my ribcage.

'Oh, come on now,' she hissed when she noticed I was crying. 'You've just had a baby.' As if she hadn't been harsh enough already, she then sprayed the open wounds with what I can only describe as some version of anti-freeze, adding stingingly to my pain.

And, at that moment, it all became clear – just how bad the treatment had been from beginning to end. How I had not been cared for, let alone listened to. How there was this general expectation – even from healthcare providers who looked like me – for me to be strong and silent, or grin and bear it. The huffs and puffs from midwives had not been my imagination. Unwarranted comments like, 'Hurry this one along', were not one-offs. Feeling unwell and not having my symptoms taken seriously was not a one-off experience.

In 2018, some five years after Esmé was born, a report was published which helped me make sense of my experience. The MBRRACE-UK report (which is used as a tool to gather data, learn lessons and inform maternity care in the UK and Ireland) exposed the horrific statistic that, in the UK, black women are five times more likely to die in childbirth than any other race. A bit like when the raised lump on my lower abdomen finally burst open, this report was proof that it wasn't all in my head and, like many other black women who felt as though they had been treated unfairly in pregnancy and childbirth, I clung to this reveal as if it were a Bible.

But another similarity between this report and the Bible is that not all are willing to believe its content. Most healthcare professionals I have spoken to since have consistently tried to put this shocking statistic down to the fact that pregnant black women are more likely to fall prey to pregnancy-related illnesses which then lead to death. Whilst I'm not educated to speak on the science behind our bodies, I am experienced enough to attest to the fact that this is not the only reason. In my opinion, a lot of this comes down to both conscious or unconscious bias, which is in part supported by the fact that the NHS is a product of a society governed by white supremacy which is willing to uphold racist values as long as nobody blows the whistle.

The day before I was discharged, the room once again filled with medical professionals. This time it was to offer an apology. Whilst they couldn't be sure as to why my wound became infected, they readily admitted to there being a long list of 'inconsistencies' and behaviour from staff which 'fell far below' the NHS standard. Sheepishly, the same doctor who had broken my waters now handed Bode some pamphlets that showed us how to make a formal complaint through the

NHS PALS service. I can't remember what Bode told them, but I'm pretty sure it isn't printable, so that's perhaps for the best.

Almost a month later, as I finally went back to a baby girl who didn't know me, I could find no words for how I had been treated or how I was feeling and, not unexpectedly, this went on to impact my mental health.

But, as with most things that we truly need, the words would find me.

When I think back to how I was treated, it makes me shiver. I came this close to not being a mother to Esmé. And with superstars like Beyoncé and Serena Williams also expressing their experience of such mistreatment – albeit in America – I think it's pertinent to note that money doesn't erase your blackness. There are stereotypical tropes in place that continue to be perpetuated and silence those being targeted.

I've written countless articles and have spoken on almost as many podcasts, panels and even the national evening news, in an attempt to keep such an urgent problem like black babies having a 121% increased risk of being stillborn at the forefront of people's minds. In mid-2019, I heavily promoted a petition which I and others were hoping would prompt the government to investigate and address why black mothers don't seem to receive the same level of care as their white counterparts. And whilst the campaign was shared by a collective social media following of over eight MILLION people, the petition was closed due to the recent general election with a measly thirty thousand signatures. It needed at least 100,000 signatures to be considered for debate, and the numbers spoke for themselves. Black mothers' lives still don't matter. But at least I'm still alive to tell you that.

6

(SENTI)MENTAL TINGS

NHS Digital data shows that detention rates under the Mental Health Act during 2017–18 were four times higher for people in the 'Black' or 'Black British' group than those in the 'White' group.

Once back home, I struggled to settle into a routine with Esmé. She preferred to sleep all day and cry all night, and I resented that Bode wasn't around for any of it. During the day he had to go to work and by dusk, he said he needed a full night's sleep to perform well the next day. Most evenings he made it home for bath time at 6pm, so that became his thing. But in the unlikely event that he was running late, Esmé would not wait. We had worked hard to get her into a strict routine, and if she sensed that her bath was running behind schedule, all hell was bound to break loose. So, on those days it was all on me. I tried my best to just get on with it, but I didn't know how. The only thing I knew about being a mother was that it could send you mad.

This went way back.

I was five or six when I first heard the word 'depression'.

I don't know what made me check on my mother that day. It was the middle of the afternoon and it just seemed so unlike her to sleep during the day.

'Mummy. Mummy!' I called, gently shaking her shoulder.

Her eyes rolled back and she groaned a little, but she wasn't making much sense.

'Mummy!' I shouted. Even though I was young, I knew something was wrong. As she slumped onto her side, I ran to the phone and stabbed the number nine button three times, just like I'd seen on TV.

Soon, my tiny body was wobbling on a stool as I tried to pronounce all of the medication in the cupboard I was never allowed to open. The lady on the other end of the phone asked if I could reach the lock on the front door – which I could. She asked me to check on Mum to see if she was breathing and then come back to the phone to tell her, and then go and check her again. This went on until the ambulance arrived. I was frightened the people with the stretcher would think I had killed her.

Later, as she was placed in the back of an ambulance, I overheard my nan (whose number I knew off by heart and was able to give to the operator) speaking with the ambulance man.

'Yes, she has overdosed before,' Nan said quietly. 'She suffers from depression quite badly.'

The next time I saw my dad, I asked him what depression was. My dad was a no-nonsense man who, in a situation like this, wouldn't try to childproof the topic.

'Listen, Cand,' he said. 'Depression isn't a real thing. It's supposed to mean when you're a bit down or sad, but I don't believe in it. I think it's just an excuse for those of us who don't want to face reality.'

It wouldn't be until years later that I would get a full grasp on what he was saying, but as young as I was, I somehow understood it to be that he didn't believe my mother was actually ill; he just thought she didn't want to be a grown-up or even a mother. And as I grew up, I realised it wasn't just my mum this was happening to. Everywhere I looked, other black women were struggling with their mental health. By the time I was in secondary school it became clear that many of my black friends knew about their mothers being sectioned or having to depend on antidepressants to make it through the day. One of my closest friends didn't really have a mother at all. She never seemed conscious. And in order for him and his sister to not be taken into care, he never spoke of it – he just became a mother and father himself. I had another friend whose mother never actually left the house. She was always in bed with the curtains drawn, allowing the darkness to swallow her whole.

It wasn't just mothers. On the road I grew up on, many

black people seemed to be struggling with their mental health. Two men who happened to be brothers killed themselves due to hearing voices. The first brother hung himself in the backyard and his mother found him the next morning, and the second one jumped out a window from a high-rise flat in front of his very young son. Now their father is often seen muttering to himself.

I started to see that my father's thoughts were echoed by the community around me. Black people just didn't seem to want to accept that depression and struggles with mental health could be a reality. Even though, all around me, it was clear that people were struggling. Seeing these things made me disagree with my own father's opinions very strongly.

Honestly, now I think about it, I knew no sprightly, happy, joyful black mothers. They all seemed to be living each day hoping to make it to the end with everything still in order. As for me, the version of motherhood that had been sold to me was a bit like the Bugaboo. It revolved around glossy women who were on top of it all, who were very, VERY happy spending days breastfeeding or pureeing organic vegetables into ice cube trays or feet painting or messy play. It was all horizontal striped T-shirts and shiny bobs. And although none of this suited me, I still wanted what they were selling. But my mental health had other plans for me.

I think what made things worse was that, all my life, I'd faced my fair share of demons, although none of them had been addressed by anyone with enough letters after their name. I'd found ways to self-medicate and distract myself so that I never had to admit that my mind was exhausted. Ever since I'd seen my mother in Maudsley Hospital, a psychiatric hospital in London, I'd made a silent promise to never let myself end up in a place like that. Because mental illness had always been positioned as either – at best – being a drama queen or – at worst – being possessed by a demonic spirit that needed to be cast out with the help of plentiful litres of holy water and thirty per cent of your net income up for tithe.

It would take years for me to understand that things didn't need to be so black and white. I'd taken on battle after battle without ever admitting that I needed help, and that didn't change after having Esmé. Being so sick after giving birth impacted me in many ways. I found the daily routine of looking after such a young baby monotonous and unful-filling. Come five in the afternoon, I would often be sitting outside the front door waiting for Bode to return from work.

'Shit, Candice, you could let me get inside first!' he'd say indignantly as I rapped my knuckles on the car window, signalling for him to wind it down.

'Listen, it's not you who has been stuck at home all day with a screaming baby!' I'd yell, handing Esmé's small body to him through the open window.

I just wasn't connecting with her and I felt very alone. All of my pre-Esmé friends were still young and having fun. No one I knew seemed to be tied down by such a demanding human. I had worked out that it was always best to wake before she did. I was out of the shower by the time Bode left for work, so that I would have Esmé's first feed ready to go when she woke up. She would eat once more before her nap at midday, after which I would have lunch and get on with household chores until she woke again between 2 and 3pm. Then it was straight into another feed and some variation of 'playtime' in front of CBeebies until the blessed show let me know it was bedtime hour.

Sandwiched between predictable tasks like nappy changes and sterilising bottles were the not so predictable things, like vomiting, and exploding nappies. By this time, the shine of a newborn had worn off and I wasn't getting too many visitors. My nan had a very full social calendar which included ball-room dancing three times a week at the same dance school she used to take me to as a child, and so I didn't see her too often. Mum lived what felt a world and a day away in Walthamstow. To get to her from where we lived in Croydon, I would have to get two buses just to get to Brixton and then sit on the tube all the way to the other end of the Victoria line, before getting another bus to my mother's door. When I assessed all that could go wrong in that almost three-hour journey, it made me rigid with fear. In fact, I was so frightened of going out with Esmé, I didn't venture outside alone with her until she was almost five months old.

I had that day planned to the letter. I would change and feed Esmé just before I left the house. I would walk the mile there and back to the high street to avoid any embarrassing meltdowns on public transport, and I would be back just in time for her next nap so she wouldn't scream the shopping centre down. Of course, the only laugh louder than God when he is watching you make plans is the sinister inner chuckle of a five-month-old baby, dead-set on fucking up your shit.

Esmé cried all the way there, all the way around the now very short shopping trip, and we both cried all of the way home. Naturally, as we approached our front door, she fell straight to sleep. At least I had got the timing right. Eyes hot with tears, I pushed her straight into the dining room and didn't even bother removing her from the pushchair.

'Mum,' I cried into the phone a few moments later. 'I don't think I can do this! Every second of my life is centred around a baby who clearly doesn't like me.'

'Candice, don't say that,' she said. 'I know it's not easy – I've done it three times. But, listen, I think you may need to see a doctor. It sounds like you need a little help . . .'

Now, I was wound up by the disastrous shopping trip, but what was she saying? I'd spent pretty much my entire lifetime trying to outrun this thing, but now whatever it was had loudly and confidently knocked at my door, and I wasn't quite sure how to deal with it turning up uninvited. But instead of sharing that with my mum, I found myself yelling at her.

'ARE YOU CALLING ME MAD?!' I screamed down the phone. 'MUM, ARE YOU CALLING ME MAD?!'

'Candice, I'm not calling you mad,' she replied calmly.

'Listen to me. I'm just saying you may need to go on anti-depressants or something. Just to help you get through this period. Becoming a new mum isn't easy. Especially after all you've been through.'

I swallowed hard. She'd hit a nerve. Since I had come home from the hospital, I hadn't given myself time to think about how differently things would've played out if Esmé hadn't fallen asleep on me that night. More than likely, the sepsis would have poisoned my bloodstream and I would have died. But I feared that if my mind went there, it perhaps wouldn't come back. I was also feeling prickly when it came to Esmé's clear – to me, anyway – preference for my mum, which didn't surprise me considering the first few weeks of her life was spent in her care. I felt silly for thinking it, as she was still so young, but it seemed as if she didn't even want to get to know me, her own mother. I was angry at the medical incompetence that had led to the lack of bonding between us, at a time when we both needed it most.

It also didn't help that Bode was really putting the pressure on to get me to sue the hospital.

'No, we have to do something,' he said one evening. 'They have to be held accountable.'

I bit my tongue. I didn't have the energy to fight depression, let alone the NHS.

'Would you just drop it?' I sighed. 'No one else had to go through what I went through, OK? I don't have the energy, and unless you're sitting on a lottery win you're not telling

me about, we really don't have the money, so just back off!'
I huffed.

I hated that he kept pushing it. His constant banging on
about how the hospital had wronged us did nothing for my
mental health. It also didn't help that I felt I couldn't admit
to feeling weak. That's not something I ever saw women who
looked like me do. We are never given the space to say we
feel that we can't do any more. In fact, we are actively trained
and encouraged to do the complete opposite.

To help illustrate how much black women take on, I use
my pyramid analogy. Stay with me whilst I break this down.

First, imagine a pyramid.

At the top of the pyramid are white men – obviously.
Just below them are white women. Below them falls every
other race apart from black and, at the very bottom of it,
we have black men. And black women? We aren't actually
on the pyramid at all. Where are we, I hear you ask? We
are the invisible pillars entrenched in the bitter soil helping
the pyramid stay upright. We are always in service. Always
available. Always taking on too much. Always providing,
performing and being polite.

Because this was the example I had, I very much struggled to admit defeat. I allowed the weeks to roll on in a wave
of monotony and sadness as I tried to stay mentally upright
enough to remember to brush my teeth and take care of
Esmé. It has to be said that, upon reflection, at my eight-week
check-up (which was delayed due to the fact I'd been so ill),

the doctor never once asked about how I felt in my state of mind. It was all about my physical well-being, a tick-box process to ensure that my body was in good working order and that I wouldn't get pregnant in the next few months. And now, considering the data surrounding postnatal depression, and specifically how black women are more likely to need help with their mental health, this is a little worrying, to say the least.

So, I was paddling very, very hard to keep it together, but soon – inevitably – it all came to a head.

I can't even remember what Bode and I were arguing about, but on that particular night, the argument was spectacular. No doubt it had something to do with who wasn't getting enough sleep, or maybe it was about someone not taking a shitty nappy outdoors (word of advice: always, always spend a few extra pounds on a lock-scent nappy bin). Whatever it was, we were going for it.

'You just don't understand meeeeeee!' I screamed and, with a swiftness usually reserved for a jungle cat, I reached for the small TV which sat on an ugly wooden stand and, aiming straight for his head, lunged it across the bedroom.

'Fuuuuuuck!' he yelled, ducking just in time for the TV to connect with the wall behind him, as it hit the floor with a thud.

I stormed out the bedroom, out the front door and ran onto the street, sobbing uncontrollably. It was like I had no control over my own body. After five or so minutes, Bode came out and practically lifted me back into the house, begging me to calm down.

'Listen, listen to me, Candice,' he said. 'I really need you to get help now. This is out of control. You are being so moody and snappy, and I don't want you taking it out on the wrong person.'

By 'person', I knew he meant Esmé. And here's the thing: I want to say that I would have never harmed a hair on her head. But that wouldn't be entirely true. There'd been times in that period that I'd let her cry a little longer than I should, or I hadn't been as soothing as I should have been. And although I assumed I would never hurt her, I didn't want to tempt fate.

Later that evening, my grandad called. Bode had called my mum to let her know about my latest wobble and she had called Grandad. It must have been an emergency in their eyes, because calling Grandad is our family's version of signalling an SOS.

'Now listen, Boobie. We just want you to be OK.' His voice was gentle but firm. 'Sometimes a woman is a little off-kilter once she's had a baby. Hormones can be a bugger. There is no harm in going to the doctor and seeing what can be done to level you out.' I would always listen to Grandad, not just because I respect him like a father, but because he himself is very open about his own battles with depression. Up until this very day, he encourages everyone to have a good cry, including himself. Whether triggered by a charity advert on TV or lamenting on what he feels he lost after the divorce with my nan, Grandad will cry and tussle with his feelings publicly. He is a rare gem.

Admittedly, throwing the TV had scared me, and I knew I'd reached some sort of tipping point, so the very next morning, I called my GP surgery.

'Unfortunately, we don't have any appointments available for the next three weeks,' the receptionist said, clearly unmoved by my desperate tone of voice.

This was not surprising, although no one was yet admitting that the NHS was being strangled to death by budget cuts. Even though we had moved boroughs countless times when I was younger, we had always gone to the same doctor's surgery. Stockwell Group Practice was the only place I'd known, and I'd known one doctor there in particular better than others because he was both my mother's and grandad's GP. Dr Lee was a petite South Asian man who had a very no-nonsense manner but a huge regard for the time patients needed in his care. Almost every day the surgery would have to close late because he couldn't care less for the new rules which dictated speed over service. He would spend at least half an hour with each patient, trying to get to the bottom of why they had called in the first place. Watching how he cared for my mother's poor mental health and didn't shy away from topics like race and class when explaining certain ailments had been quite something.

But he had long gone and the leisurely, almost therapeutic-like setting that he had provided was a thing of the past. Now the doctors there – who were admittedly under pressure, underpaid and undervalued – spoke so fast it's as if their tongues were in Grand Prix competitions. They seemed to be solely focused on getting through patients as quickly as possible and there was no time for a catch-up or discussion that delved into your diagnosis. It was in, out, in, out, shake it all about.

But now, I couldn't even get in to get out to shake it all about.

'OK, no worries, thanks, bye,' I mumbled, hanging up the phone.

I know I should have made the appointment, but three weeks felt an awfully long time just to say that I felt, well, awful. I hadn't thought it through, but should Bode or Grandad ask, I would perhaps lie and say I booked the appointment just to keep them both off my back for a while.

Later that evening I told my mum what had happened.

'Listen, I know I shouldn't,' she said. 'But when I see you, I'm going to give you some of my stuff.'

By now, I knew that 'stuff' meant her happy pills. Since the episode I had witnessed when I was knee-high, she had always been on antidepressants. When she was feeling good the dose would come down, and once or twice she had tried and failed to go cold turkey. But a bit like elevator music, the pills were always there lingering in the background. I didn't even have the strength to argue with her. Plus, I had little doubt that my GP wouldn't have done much different and slapped me on the pills. My silence was met as compliance and, true to her word, next time I saw her she hastily stuffed a box of them into my palm.

'Only take one. I take two, but I don't think you need that much.' She looked me up and down. 'And this is just between us, you hear?' she said, without room for any argument.

I agreed with that one thousand per cent. Shit, if Bode knew that I was taking my mother's mental-health medication, he would think I'd lost the plot. But at this point it was clear to me that I was not 'myself' and I was willing to do anything to shake this dark cloud. Without hesitating, I grabbed a tumbler from the cupboard, filled it with cool water directly from the kettle and took one of the tablets.

'Fluoxetine.' I read the word aloud to nobody in particular and naively waited for them to take effect. Of course, nothing happened.

I must have communicated my impatience, as Mum laughed. 'You have to wait a few days, love,' she said. 'After that, you will wonder how on earth you lived a life without them.'

And she was bang on. By the third day, I was able to have a conversation with Bode without losing my temper. By the fifth day, Esmé's crying didn't bother me, and seven or so days later I decided I would take Esmé to one of those mother and baby groups. Between you and me, I had absolutely no mummy friends and I was very jealous of those women on the Mumsnet forums who constantly referenced what a 'saviour' NCT had been for them.

'That's great for you,' I thought. But our financial net had been just about wide enough to catch a second-hand buggy – albeit the Rolls-Royce of buggies, whatever-hand – and other essentials. Paying to do downward-facing-heavily-pregnant-dog with some strangers was just not a financial priority.

Also, there was Instagram. I had an account I rarely used, but since Esmé had been born I'd found myself posting and browsing on there more. In the 3am fog of the night feeds, I'd search the motherhood hashtag and follow random British mummy accounts. I wasn't talking to anyone and they surely didn't know I existed, but my heavy eyelids and mush-like brain thought it was a great idea.

Until it wasn't. It once again reiterated that my kind of motherhood wasn't one anyone seemed interested in selling. No black British women were even coming up when I searched for these tags. But desperation made me look past our differences and cling to slithers of similarity. Longingly, I looked on at what seemed to be perfect snapshots from these mummy meet-ups, wishing for a few seconds of what they had. This new-found, heavily medicated mental clarity, albeit still in the very early days, really made me admit to myself that what I was missing was good old-fashioned, real-life friendship. Sure, I had my sister, but she was still so young and carefree that I couldn't ever reach her on the phone before 1pm, because she'd still be asleep. And the few friends I did have who had kids had all long since passed the nappy stage and I could tell they had absolutely no desire to relive poonamies and potty training. I was an island and I had to accept that this was no good for me, and no good for Esmé.

So, I decided that the next day would be that day. Time had taught me not to put pressure on either myself or the baby, but the nearest baby group was only a ten-minute walk away at a time she would usually be awake anyhow. If neither of us was feeling it, I would leave. All I had to do was get to the baby group and then take it from there.

'So, any plans tomorrow?' Bode asked out of sheer habit that night. Whereas usually this tired-ass question would have pissed me off, today I felt a flicker of . . . excitement. Since the town centre scenario I hadn't left the house with Esmé to go further than the corner shop, and that was only if the gas and electric meter needed topping up. But tonight was different.

'Actually, yes,' I replied, a bit smugly. 'I'm going to a mother and baby group tomorrow.'

His eyes grew wide with shock, but he composed himself as he tried to replace surprise with support.

'Oh, word? That's good! I think that will be great for both of you, and you seem a lot more relaxed these days.'

Suddenly I felt as if he could see right through me, and I felt myself trying to shrink to not be seen.

'Really?' I asked, trying to keep my voice even.

'Yeah, I don't know what's happening, but I think the baby blues may be on their way out.'

'Maybe.' I sighed, but I couldn't help but reflect on how bad this could get. I was thirteen when I first stepped foot into a psychiatric unit to visit my mother. I hadn't forgotten how unrecognisable she had appeared to me, lying in her bed limp and disconnected, her eyes vacant. All she could do when I asked her questions was groan at me.

I kept taking the antidepressants. They made me feel as though I was walking on air. There were a few times I would skip a dose just to see if they were really working their magic, and I don't know if it was all in my head, but without them, I felt unstable. Whenever I was running low, I would beg my mum to get me another packet, both of us perhaps unaware of how this wasn't the best way to go about things. By now Esmé and I had settled into a wonderful routine and the better weather made more outside activity possible, which helped encourage me to get out and about more. Much like the day Bode had called me.

It was a warmer day than usual when I felt my phone vibrate in my back pocket. 'Candice,' said Bode, and I could tell by his tone that something was off.

'Yeah, what's up?' I asked, doing that very awkward dance of trying not to drop my phone whilst pushing a pushchair.

'Candice, I've just found some tablets – fluoxetine,' said Bode, his voice like lead. 'Like, what the fuck is this?'

I felt my lungs deflate like a helium balloon in a cactus field.

I wanted to both defend myself and tell him to fuck off, but instead I felt my voice drop low and my tone became defensive.

'Can't you read? They're clearly antidepressants.'

'Of course I know what they are, but when were you going to tell me?'

I kissed my teeth.

'And now, when would you have had time to listen?' I said, feeling my voice rise again. 'I'm on my way home. I'll see you when I get there.'

I walked home slowly, trying to calm myself down. I already understood that his line of questioning would only be coming from a place of caring, but it was hard to express how tight and wound-up I felt, without us having a full-blown argument.

When I did finally make it home, he was waiting for me on the doorstep. Silently he helped me get the buggy inside, closing the dining-room door behind him so Esmé could continue napping.

'Before you even start,' I said, pulling up a kitchen chair and allowing it to catch the entirety of my weight. 'I am only going to tell you once: you're not my dad.'

Bode had an air about him which annoyed me some-times. One of the reasons I had fallen in love with him was because he had the ability to take the lead, but it also meant that whenever he had felt I had done something wrong he always came across as parental – which triggered my daddy issues no end.

'I just don't know what you were thinking,' he said, the exasperation in his voice piercing me. 'If the doctor had prescribed them, you wouldn't have hidden them. Why are you hiding this from me? Who gave them to you?'

All of a sudden, the floor became fascinating. I didn't want to meet his gaze.

'It's like you don't listen,' I said. 'I said for months I'd been struggling. You're never home. I'm with that child all day, every day, and then even come the weekend your head is stuck in your laptop because you're consumed with your stupid job. Yes, your job keeps the rent paid, but what about us? What about me?' It was only the jerkiness of my shoulders which alerted me to the fact that I was crying.

'And you think this has been easy for me?' he said, and I could hear he too was crying. I looked at him. 'Candice, you almost died, and I think we are all still in shock from that.' There were a few moments of silence where we both tried to compose ourselves. 'But you can't just take a medicine that wasn't prescribed for you. I'm sorry, I won't allow it.'

'Just say it! Just say it, Bode,' I demanded. 'Say that you don't believe in depression! You're just like my dad. He always thought that those with poor mental health were either lazy or living on another planet, and that is not true!'

'Candice!' Bode exclaimed. 'I'm NOT saying that.'

'So, what the fuck are you saying, Bode? Tell me, please?'

'I am saying that this isn't you and I won't watch these feelings swallow you whole. I just won't do it.'

As if on cue, Esmé began to wail and she temporarily distracted us both, giving me time to think things through.

A temporary truce ensued, during which we both had time to think. Later that evening, I laid my cards on the table.

'Bode, you're right,' I told him. 'I shouldn't have done that, and I will stop taking the pills, but I also want you to understand that I need help. I feel like you only hear what you want to hear and see what you want to see, and I can't continue like this.'

'Agreed,' he said. 'But I think what you need to do is go to see your own GP and really talk about how you're feeling, OK?'

'OK,' I relented.

'Do you promise?'

I drew a cross over my heart and then pretended to die and we both burst out laughing.

Two weeks later, I finally got an appointment to see my GP. Having only just returned from maternity leave, she was very understanding, but funnily enough, when she offered me antidepressants, I didn't want to take them. All I'd ever really wanted was to be heard. Bode had heard me and his response had been so different from the one I'd feared, and the doctor had heard me and offered me a solution. But that wasn't the solution I wanted. And so, over time, I weaned myself off the antidepressants I'd got from Mum and tried my hardest to focus on getting out more. I joined a gym and regularly tried to go out with my sister or other friends just to remind myself that there was more to me than just being Esmé's mum. I also admitted to myself that this would always be an uphill battle and when the time was right, I would have to get some deep therapy to help unpack all the past trauma which the pressures of motherhood were now bringing to the forefront.

But the most important thing was that I was talking and taking responsibility for my own mental health, and for me, that was a small win I could cling to when there were more clouds than rainbows.

7

YOUNG, GIFTED AND STABBED

According to the Office for National Statistics (as reported in January 2020), 15,080 knife offences were recorded in the capital during the twelve months to the end of last September, amounting to a two per cent rise on the previous year.

'Matthew wasn't involved in gang activity. He was the only one who always told me to stay away from that life. Matthew was killed on his front doorstep. His mother found him dying and held him until the ambulance arrived. She has no one left now. How could you do that to a mother? What sort of heart do you have? What burns me the most is that it's always the blacks killing the blacks. We're meant to be brothers but the way it's going it's like we hate each other, and I don't know why.'
(Friend of murdered Matthew Kitandwe, who was eighteen when he died, as reported by VICE in the documentary On A Knife Edge*).*

When the grime artist Stormzy appeared on the main stage at Glastonbury in June 2019, he was the first solo black British headliner in the festival's history. He opened his set with a previously unpublicised interview with past headliner Jay-Z, and the exchange shone a light on how unusual and disruptive their appearances were. Since its conception, Glastonbury, much like most of Britain, has silently prided itself on being for a certain sort of person – an almost-always-not-black person whose musical preferences never include rap. And yet both men found themselves centre stage at this iconic British institution more comfortably home to moss-coloured wellies and boho festival attire.

I'd missed the live performance, but the next morning I watched it on iPlayer on the 10.40am train to Birmingham. It was the hottest day of the year so far, with temperatures predicted to soar to an uncomfortable 31 degrees, and the mood on board was tetchy. But I was exhilarated, and as I rapped aloud to Stormzy's set, I shut off the world around me, not giving one fuck about who my public joy disturbed. Because, I thought, as I watched him striding out onto the raised platform, it's about time. As the showman himself has since rapped, 'What a fucking time to be a black Brit.' What a time, indeed.

But this wasn't just about being on the stage at Glastonbury. Stormzy's attire told another story; his top half was weighed down by a stab vest, its front decorated with a dripping Union Jack flag which had been decorated by none other than the private and prolific artist, Banksy. And this took my breath away. For, even in a moment where he must have felt at the highest point in his career, he was unwavering in his intent to remind people, more specifically white people, that bodies like his – young, black, male bodies – are under constant threat.

The stats backed him up. At the time of writing, the rate of knife crime, specifically in London, is at its highest. Working backwards, it was reported by the Metropolitan police that 2018 had been the bloodiest year in almost a decade, with the murder toll capping at 134, and by June 2019, thirty-five lives had already been lost due to knife crime. 2019 was not to be outdone as, by the end of it, it would supersede the violence of 2018. Even more alarmingly, the flow of blood seeping through London streets shows no sign of slowing any time soon, as illustrated by the statistic at the top of this chapter.

When I was growing up, we were all very familiar with the names Stephen Lawrence and Damilola Taylor. Even today, the murder of Stephen Lawrence in 1993 stands like a neon flag planted in recent British history to remind us all of the insidious and deadly racism that not only operates within the hearts of the racist murderers themselves, but also continues to permeate the Metropolitan police force. I was a child when Stephen was murdered, but I was fully aware of his death and the many inconsistencies in the investigation, because Stephen's story became akin to disturbing folklore within the black community. It was a blindingly obvious example of how much black British lives didn't matter to the police force. But despite that, as I grew up, Stephen's murder somehow felt like an unfortunate, isolated incident removed from my current reality.

Damilola Taylor's murder on the streets of Peckham in November 2000 hit a little closer to home, literally. Peckham was one 345 bus ride away from where I grew up in Brixton and was often a pit-stop on Saturday mornings after trips to East Street Market in Southwark. Damilola Taylor was a mere ten years old when he was attacked on his way home from Peckham Library. Ten. Even today, at a time so riddled with bloodshed, that age would make anyone take a sharp breath. At the time of his death, he was only two years younger than me. It was a murder that grabbed headlines and hearts simultaneously, and honestly, in hindsight, it seems like the PG prelude to the 18+ horror story we now endure today. But back then, the situation felt so unique it almost seemed abstract, so unbelievable it was. Knife crime wasn't the omnipresent beast it is now.

Apart from Stephen Lawrence, Damilola Taylor was the only other victim my friends and I could put a face to, and our Brixton-based family members became firm in reminding us that no good could come from hanging around Peckham, as it had now been pinpointed as the London hotspot for murderous activity. So, outside of this space, my friends and I felt relatively safe. When we went out, we never, ever thought about the evening ending in bloodshed. Sure, there may have been a scuffle between two boys, and perhaps you would see a track of weave decorating the pavements where two girls had given into their animalistic sides and gone for each other – usually for no other reason than one 'screw facing' another for too long – but that would always be the end of it.

But this was soon to change, and by the time I was eighteen, the whole of London – not just Peckham – was suffering from terrifying gun issues. Drive-bys were becoming the fashionable way to end a dispute, and arguments about who 'ran the streets' in certain postcodes had begun to spill out into full-blown wars. I'd been in nightclubs where machetes had been wielded and at parties where knives appeared, and I'd seen the rise in crime that was a direct result of drug trafficking. By the time I was in secondary school, gang-affiliated boys instructed to protect postcodes and sell drugs – primarily to the white middle class, who simply wanted to 'take the edge off' at the end of a long week – now used firearms as their primary way of making others see their point of view. Guns had now become such a problem that Operation Trident – which was originally set up in 1998 by the black community and positioned as a community-led initiative in conjunction with the Met police – was a very well established unit and at the centre of almost every violent headline.

But, as with all matters, when you pay too much attention to one aspect it gives another problem space to mutate, and that's exactly what happened with knife crime. Easier to come by and not yet under the scrutiny of the Met, knives – and, in turn, knife crime – have become a cancer for which there seems to be no cure. By 2011, 30,000 knife offences were committed across England and Wales, and by 2017 that was up by a further 5,000.

2017 was also the year I found out I was expecting a second child – our son, RJ. By then, we were living in a tiny rented flat in South Croydon. I mean, it was so dinky that I think even Tinkerbell would have had a right giggle. But, due to rising rents pushing out many die-hard Londoners who wanted to stay in the city by any means possible, this Zone Five cubicle with a Juliet balcony that neither she nor Romeo could have actually fitted on was deemed as 'luxury'. And, for a while, it was. We had taken out a horrifyingly high-interest loan that enabled us to put down the deposit, first and last month's rent, for square footage so reduced that if you took a shit, the whole block knew.

Whilst we weren't completely out of the woods in regard to our finances, we were doing better. After a short-lived stint working for a publishing company, I had jacked it all in to concentrate on raising Esmé full-time and trying to get a media career off the ground. In between that I had reignited my love of baking to help supplement Bode's income. On the busier weeks, our tiny kitchen would be filled to the brim with baking utensils, but it did mean that I could bring in anything up to £500. It wasn't perfect, but it was working. So, when my period was late and I had finally gotten around to taking a test, I wasn't arrested by financial fear like I had been with Esmé. And in that regard, nor was Bode. He was worried for a different reason.

'Right,' said Bode. 'I've been thinking. If we're going to have another baby, we are going to have to leave London.'

He'd been talking like this for some time. A year or so previously we'd looked into moving out of London, but it had just made no sense. Yes, the air was cleaner, the rental property prices were cheaper and there didn't seem to be violent crime in these postcodes every day, but they weren't London. And because of that, I had come up with every excuse in the world as to why leaving just wasn't an option.

'It's so far from work. I have a pretty good customer base here.'

'We have no family outside of London.'

'I checked Deliveroo and they don't even operate off ends.'

Truth be told, I was scared. Firstly, although I'd lived in ten different addresses in twenty-seven years, they were all within this tiny pocket of the UK that I called home. I knew all there was to know about London, from how to deal with obtuse cabbies, to which Morley's fried chicken eatery did the best barbecue ribs. Beyond that, London was a multicultural melting pot which offered a space where I felt I could actually breathe and succeed. I didn't want to be tolerated; I wanted to be celebrated. And I had no idea what reaction would await us should we decide to take a risk on middle England.

I had no intention of leaving my home, my comfort zone.

But, now that we were having another child, something way down in my intuition knew he was right, because if the baby I was carrying happened to be a boy, there was no way in hell I wanted him to be raised in an environment that actively pursued to end his life before he got a chance to dictate how it was lived.

'You know what?' I sighed. 'I completely agree with you.'

'Really?!' Bode smiled (and whenever he smiles, I grow envious because he has the most perfect teeth).

It's funny, because I instinctively knew that I was having a boy. As, in fact, did both Esmé and my mother. It's the good old juju again. Months before I'd even conceived, one of Esmé's then nursery teachers cornered me one chilly evening. 'So, I hear congratulations are in order,' she said brightly.

I followed her eyeline and looked down at my tummy and back up at her and laughed. 'But I'm not pregnant,' I said, as her changing skin tone began to betray her embarrassment.

'I'm so, so sorry,' she said. 'It's just that Esmé seemed so adamant she was having a baby brother. I should have been a little more sensitive.'

Later that evening, as I relayed this exchange to Bode, he looked at me carefully. 'Are you sure you're not? You know that Esmé won't say something unless she means it.'

'Yeah, I know,' I said. 'It's weird. And remember, Mum did dream that she was coming to our new house to look after a baby boy.'

I had been adamant that Esmé was going to be a boy. So

adamant that, for the first trimester, I referred to the baby as a 'he' and, until we found out otherwise, only purchased clothes from the boy section of Primark. As I said earlier, I was fearful of raising a girl, but what I didn't know then, and have come to understand through working with a therapist, is that I had a fear of having a girl because I had subconsciously believed that I didn't have the tools needed to be the mother to a female child. But at the time, I said things like, 'I don't know, boys just seem easier.' I was so locked into the idea of having a boy that when I went along to the twenty-week scan, I was solely consumed with my hopes being confirmed.

'What is it?!' I pressed impatiently as my eyes swung between the sonographer and the blurry-looking image they had assured me was a baby.

'It's a girl!' She smiled, sure that she had delivered me the best news since Barack Obama was announced as the President.

My face fell and pregnancy exhaustion meant that I was too tired to even hide it. 'Oh, OK. Thanks,' I mumbled, fighting back tears.

Due to a work meeting, Bode hadn't been able to make the appointment, so my mum had come with me. She locked eyes with me and gave me her 'don't you dare' look, which black mothers seem to be famous for. Even at my big, big age, I knew to suck the tears back up.

'What was that?' Mum asked as we made our way out of the hospital and walked along the Thames path, the breeze brisk and refreshing. 'Listen, I know you wanted a boy, but you have to be thankful that your child is happy and healthy.'

I felt the tears well up again before I even noticed I was crying. Pregnant or not, I knew better than to argue with my mum in public.

She approached my face with a clean tissue, dabbing gently so as not to ruin my make-up. 'Come on, Candice, this is meant to be a joyous occasion.'

And, of course, she was right. Esmé had come into my life and illuminated it so brightly that any early ill feelings I had had about her not being a boy were firmly left behind.

And now here I was pretty much panicking about the thought of raising a boy in inner-city London. I'd learned a lot from my brother, who is fourteen years younger than me, meaning that he is currently part of the generation which finds themselves to be most embroiled in the violence all around us.

Just like there was garage and then later grime music, which felt as if it were created solely to narrate my every feeling when I was a teen, there is a new sound on the scene these days by the name of drill. Like all new genres that have come before it – rap in particular – drill music has had to shoulder the brunt of being the alleged main reason as to why these children seek to hack each other to pieces. Countless lackadaisical news reports have accused drill of being the reason why young boys are intent on getting more points on their violent scoreboards. (It is public knowledge that there is a scoreboard system which is used within gangs. The more ferociously you can harm someone from an opposing gang – otherwise known as the 'Opps' – the higher the scores you receive. For example, stabbing someone in the head would earn you fifty points, whereas stabbing them in the leg would be worth ten. The total points earned and held by each gang of course dictates which gang could currently boast about running tings.) This level of violence isn't new, and nor is the ability to taunt the Opps by going back to back on diss tracks.

But blaming a new, emerging genre of music for the reason knife crime is climbing year on year makes very little sense, considering that it was only sixteen years ago that Glasgow had a reputation for being the murder capital of Europe, with knife crime driving much of the violence in that area. Although I have yet to visit Glasgow, I'll place high bets on the fact that the knife crime there very rarely featured a black boy with a love for drill music at either end of the blade. There are mothers of all races burying their sons because of knife crime, and the sad truth is that a white boy's face on the front of the papers doesn't fit with this country's overarching need to show black people as the only ones, above or below ground, who are involved with violent crime.

Take the reporting of the murder of seventeen-year-old Jodie Chesney in March 2019. Images of Jodie hit the front page of every paper, lauding the teen as an 'angel' who 'wouldn't harm a fly'. Whilst it isn't for me to dispute Jodie's character, what was clear to me was the blatant bias when it came to how Jodie's murder was being presented to the general public. Jodie, the white girl who was stabbed to death whilst sitting in a park, was now the perfect poster child to use to show how much more valid white lives are than black. Black boys who have suffered the same fate are relegated to passport-sized images in the slimmest of columns. This was quite literally displayed for all to see when, alongside Jodie's image, a Sunday paper showed the images of two black boys' passport photos, which to the undiscerning eye looked like police mugshots. It looked like they were Jodie's killers when in fact, upon reading deeper into the article, those two black boys had also lost their lives in a senseless way.

Even though this current spike in knife crime is unprecedented, the continued response from the government and the Met police force is still a weak, two-pronged approach: they assure us they will put more police on the streets and they will become more heavy-handed in regards to stop and searches. This, of course, has been a source of aggravation within communities who already find it hard to trust the police, for a variety of complex reasons, including the institutionally racist handling of the Stephen Lawrence murder and most recently the Mark Duggan case, which was one of the causes of the now-infamous 2011 London riots.

Police brutality isn't just a sickness our American cousins are suffering from; it's far closer to home than we could imagine. From more vintage atrocities such as Christopher Alder, who died whilst in police custody, and Cynthia Jarrett, whose death during a police raid on her home sparked the infamous Broadwater Farm riot, to the more recent deaths of Rashan Charles and Edson Da Costa, who both reportedly swallowed substances and/or packages before being arrested, we must constantly remind ourselves that the reality that you are more likely to be killed by the police because you are black is just as real this side of the water.

Such deaths have, of course, provided the most perfect petri dish for ill feeling to metaphorically mature in. The turbulent relationship between black youths and the police that was already rooted in mistrust has exploded into all-out war, with the young black men and boys incorrectly made targets of haphazard solutions. It's like decorating a gangrenous limb with plasters in the hope they will miraculously reverse any damage done. Instead, any respect the youth should have had for the feds is now completely null and void.

I was witness to this most recently at Notting Hill Carnival. A handsome and quiet black boy, who seemed to be no more than seventeen, alighted the train with two friends at the same time as me, my mother and sister. Suddenly, he was pulled aside by six police officers. Six. We told them that he had not even yet set foot into the carnival, but they said that Section 60 was in place, giving them liberty to stop anyone perceived as a 'potential threat', and they found the fact that he was wearing a tracksuit on a very hot day to be 'peculiar'.

Instinctively both my sister and I took out our phones and, with the boy's permission, began recording the stop and search. It was all we could do. He could have been our brother, and in a sense he was our brother. After ten minutes, they let him go because they found him not to be in possession of anything illegal. Visibly shaken, the young boy thanked us as he tried to put on a brave face.

One might assume that this was a unique situation, but as the day of festivities rolled on, it became clear that the police were using Section 60 to wield power over only a certain sect of teenagers. Just before we left, we saw seven black boys being forced to face a boarded-up house, raise their hands above their heads and spread their legs. Should they resist, they were threatened with arrest. I tried hard to fight back the tears. If you continuously treat a section of humanity as animals, how long do you think it will be before they act accordingly?

In order to work on the right response, we need to look at the root causes and the reasons why violent crime is as high as it is. Whilst I appreciate this would perhaps take me a further two books, it's worth outlining what I believe to be at play here.

Whilst some see it as an excuse, I firmly believe that poverty has a massive role to play in all this destruction. Most of those in haste to write this off as a reason have perhaps never had to hide from a bailiff nor miss any meals. According to the GOV.UK website, in 2017–18 there were only 21,975 black graduates on undergraduate courses compared to a whopping number of 262,415 white students. This means that many black people enter the workforce without university degrees and become stuck in low-paid, unskilled work or zero-hour contracts with no benefits or security. And when these people become parents, they have to put more hours into making ends meet, meaning they spend less time at home. Couple this with the general ever-growing cost of childcare and extracurricular activities, providing safe, stimulating spaces outside of their children's classrooms or bedrooms can't be at the top of their priorities. When a young boy is transitioning from childhood to adolescence, I would argue that there is no other time in his life when he'd be more susceptible to peer pressure. And, given that from the offset, most of these boys have been raised in concrete, closed-in estates that offer the only affordable housing options for their already cash-strapped parents, their idea of community is limited to that within the invisible walls designed to box them in. Outside of that space, nothing else matters.

With their parents not around, these boys look for a sense of camaraderie in the streets that raised them. The only problem is that now these streets have become a playground for invisible but omnipresent drug lords, who puppeteer the older boys, or 'elders', the young ones have always looked up to. Understanding that these young boys' weak spots have always been lack of resources, be it money or adult supervision, the elders find it's far too easy to entice an eleven-year-old to 'hold' something for them for fifty pounds, especially if said eleven-year-old's parents are at work until late and so are unable to govern his choices.

And if he's never had more than the two pounds his dad has pressed into his palm each morning to help supplement his menu choices for that day, fast money will always trump consequences. Combine this with the aforementioned fact that black boys are more likely to be excluded from school, and you can quickly see how things can escalate in a deadly fashion.

To make things worse, outside resources that used to be in place where Mum or Dad fell short are slowly ceasing to exist. Most youth clubs and community centres are being boarded up due to cuts in government funding, and so these children have figuratively and literally been left out in the cold. I speak from chilling experience when I say, ain't nowhere colder than the streets – but, as I've mentioned before, this isn't an autobiography. So, let's be honest, is it that surprising that the corner boy lookout, tripling his pocket money, ends up stopping trying to succeed in a school that already labels him as problematic, and ends up graduating to a more sinister role as an elder within a gang? I don't think so. After all, everyone wants to be Top Boy.

And what about those boys who have been able to resist being groomed and initiated into a gang whose sole existence is limited to selling drugs and protecting their 'ends'? They are still at risk. Postcode wars mean that a wrong left turn here or a father asking you to run to a newsagent you aren't familiar with could end with more than the milk being spilt. I must remind people that not all of these deaths are 'deserved' (none of them ever are); some simply occur due to wrong place, wrong time.

Such a complex web of violence is frightening enough on its own. But now throw in the hype of social media and it makes this an even more heartbreaking scenario. Twenty years ago, if these children were to scrap, they would only have to prove themselves to the mates stood around them. Now, a whole world is watching. Many revenge stabbings are caught on video, then shared on platforms like Instagram and Snapchat, with the sole aim of goading the opposition, and these videos create even more reason for these boys to be seen to appear as dangerous as possible.

And to add insult to injury, the spaces around them are changing. To my eye, more money seems to be spent gentrifying the streets they've always called home than on supporting their education. Walking around my hometown of Brixton, I barely recognise it. In 2018, Brixton Market was sold for £37.3 million. London & Associated Properties said it 'has offloaded Brixton Village and Market Row to a private group of real-estate companies', as reported in the *Evening Standard*. This sale took place during the same time frame it's reported that Lambeth Academy excluded more than twenty per cent of pupils. The Department for Education exclusion figures in 2017–18 show that the school handed out at least one fixed-term exclusion to 21.7% of its students. This represents the highest fixed-term exclusion rate in South London and the third highest in London overall. But hell, at least these children now have champagne and oyster bars on their doorsteps.

Early in 2020, Mike Sheridan, Ofsted's London regional director, said in Schools Week, 'I worry about black boys in London. I worry about the numbers that are excluded and I worry about the number who are off-rolled and by themselves.' He said he worried that black boys were more likely to be the victims of serious violence in London and they were more likely to be stopped and searched by the police. He finished by stating that 'too many black boys within our system don't do well enough and we need to be willing to talk about that – we have to be willing to step up and say we need to do more'.

Without delivering a history lesson, the British Empire wouldn't exist if it were not for the pilfering of not only things like sugar, but of course the black bodies that made the growing of such riches possible. And now in a move so stealthy only the wealthy saw it coming, the rug is being pulled from beneath our feet. Despite the meteoric rise in the cost of living, most wages have stayed the same, notably for the black folk who don't have a university education and find themselves just trying to make ends meet. All this, whilst a few feet away, another artisanal coffee shop is being 'upscaled', serving hibiscus-flavoured flat whites, which, for the cost, I always imagine to be decorated with the sweat of baby Jesus. There are now two versions of London: the one I'd always known and loved – but is no longer recognisable

– and this new version which doesn't appear to want to acknowledge or respect the hard work and sacrifice of those who have spent the time building it up. This new London is willing to ignore the loss of young black life and carry on with their sophisticated cheese bars and hot yoga classes. In fact, I recently came across an article written by a woman who was not born in London but has since bought a home here, and within said article, she refers to her area as being a 'little bit stabby'. Jesus.

With my eighteen-year-old brother still living in London, my heart always, always skips a few beats whenever my mother's number flashes up on my phone, especially if it's late at night. He is the most well-mannered and funny young man I have the pleasure of knowing, but expecting the worst is maybe me trying to protect myself from the first cut of one million that many families are now trying to heal from. I know my brother is a good kid. But to believe that he is not at risk of being injured or dying from a blade is to bury my head in a bucket of ignorance that I can't afford. To be completely honest, I'd rather my brother stayed inside and didn't even visit the shops to purchase sweets. But what kind of a life is that?

He is currently taking driving lessons in between study-ing sound engineering at college. He works part-time to help supplement his many hobbies, one of which is DJ'ing. I often spy on him on Snapchat – I mean, come on, what brother wants to know their much older sister is following them on social media? – where he posts reactions to his set 'drops' at events he is DJ'ing for. To see him dripping in sweat and hypnotised by the vibes, it amazes me that not only is he talented, but he is also unrelenting in his quest to better himself at his craft. He is also a wonderful uncle. Watching him interact with the babies of the family really makes me excited to hopefully later see him step into the role of father-hood. Hopefully.

But, back in 2017, I was about to understand that the blanket of fear I draped on my brother's shoulders wasn't a unique warmth solely reserved for him. Its loving hug would extend to my baby. When we found out I was carrying a boy, I could see that, in becoming a mother to a son, I needed to take stock; because, assuming I worked night and day to keep him out of the clutches of gangs, how long would I also be able to keep the overzealous police off his back as he grew up to be the very embodiment of who they're taught to imprison? And whilst I couldn't predict the future, I could work hard to ensure that I gave my children the safest head-start possible. I could see no alternative. Unfortunately, this meant leaving the only city I had ever called home.

For the son I would give birth to, the threats were immi-nent and all-consuming. He would have to be mindful of his peers and the pressures they could put upon him. He would have to learn to live with undignified harassment from the police. I knew all too well that fleeing London wouldn't make every one of these issues magically disappear, but I'd read through the data available in its entirety and slept on the stats, and they all pointed to the fact that leaving would reduce some of those risks considerably.

The move would take all we had, and I'm not just talking about guts. A shift like this was going to cost us money we didn't have. And I would also have to be realistic about turning my back on the support systems I had come to depend on. It's here that I also have to leave space for the fact that for many black people, the idea of leaving London is a privilege. For some, their housing situation means that they have no choice but to stay put. For others, it may be because the idea of a life without the support of extended family and friends could make them feel as though they have no life at all. And there are those who may rightfully fear that moving to a less diverse community could eventually do more harm than good. Whatever their reasons are, they are valid. But when I personally allowed myself to envision the worst and imagine how much I would spend on my son's funeral, and how much I could potentially lose if we stayed put, if we took a chance on the city which was folding in around us, there was no comparison.

With this baby, just like the last, I would choose life. For him, her and us. And so off we went.

8

BROWN GIRL IN THE RING

In January 2020, BBC News Analysis
found that 'primary school exclusions for
racism in England are up by more than
forty per cent in just over a decade'.

I was running a little late to collect Esmé, which wasn't like me. A fast walk would have me at the school gates in fifteen minutes, so I picked up the pace a little, trying to ignore the beads of sweat that were already threatening to show themselves through my ice-blue shirt.

My phone rang and, like most millennials, I was already holding it, so there was no need to break stride to rifle through my pockets. It was Esmé's school calling, and I thought: that's strange. What would prompt a call so close to the end of the school day?

'Er, hello, is that Mrs Brathwaite? It's Esmé's teacher calling.'

'Yes,' I answered with some trepidation.

'Now, don't panic!' she said – and if you're a parent, you know that's code to do exactly that. All of a sudden, my heart was racing as if I were trying to go stride-for-stride with Mo Farah. 'But we've had a little incident today and unfortunately I do have to report it to you.'

Before I go on, let me kick it to you on the real. If you're the mother of a black child who lives in Britain, you are either consciously or unconsciously waiting on Two Days. Now, you won't necessarily be holding your breath waiting, because there's the in-between day-to-day navigation of getting your child or children from A to B whilst maintaining your safety, sanity and sanctuary. But, like a distant memory that wafts in and out of your consciousness, you are somewhere always waiting for these Two Days: the first is the day your offspring notices that they are black, and the second, the day someone ostracises them for that very reason.

I remember my Two Days clearly because mine came at the same time, wrapped up in one buy-one-get-one-free-type experience. I was barely seven years old, when on the number 2 bus from Crystal Palace to Brixton, a black man spoke to me. 'No, you real ugly. What man would ever want you? Yuh too black and look pon your lips, dem big-eeee?' His piled-up dreadlocks shook as he spoke.

The bus was packed, and Mum and I had taken seats separate from each other. But still, one would think with all the adults sitting around me, at least one of them would have chastised him for speaking to a child in this manner. But no one came to my defence. I swallowed my pride and pain and kept my eyes fixed ahead until it was clear he wasn't going to speak to me again. And I kept it to myself, never speaking about it until I was in my late teens, by which time, even though back then I'd known the man couldn't have been in his right mind, it had become clear that he had helped plant the seeds of feeling ugly and inferior, which society didn't hesitate to feed and water. It's important to note that the man was black. And when I share this story with other black women of my age, it is clear that first and foremost, the majority of us learned about our blackness, and our own race's particular distaste for a black that can't be hidden with 'straight hair' or 'hazel eyes', through the attitudes and actions of black men.

Even though I had sporadic moments that reminded me I wasn't in alignment with a 'type' of black which could simply be written off as 'exotic', I was still surrounded by people who looked like me. From the fellow students I attended school with, to all of the grown folk I'd bless my eyes upon during a Saturday spent pulling a shopping trolley behind my nan in East Street Market, I could see people who could provide either a current or future reflection of me, and I was able to find comfort and acceptance in that.

After having Esmé, it would be only once in a blue moon that I would glance over at her and think about the time she, too, would realise that she was black. It would catch me at the most random times – like when she announced that she and her then current best friend, who was a little white boy, were twins because they both wore glasses; how cute – but when it did, I was immediately weighed down by the reminder that I was raising a little black girl in a country where she would forever be referred to as a minority.

But, I figured, because of the multicultural community we lived in, she'd grow into her blackness the same way I did – with some difficulty, of course, but with the verbal and silent support of black people all around her. So, for a while, the reality of my fears never really had time to fester. That she'd trip and stumble into her blackness was rarely at the forefront of my mind.

Until, that is, we moved out of London to a village in the Borough of Milton Keynes. And yes, we were the only blacks in it. In fact, we were the only people of colour (Jesus, I hate that term – last time I checked not a limb in my body was green), apart from the Indian family who ran the corner shop two doors down. Their presence was a comfort, as being able to clap eyes on anyone who could be identified by the majority as 'other' allows you to breathe a little easier. But outside of that very smiley family, we were the only lick of melanin you could clap your eyes on.

We'd fallen in love with our chosen village because it felt like the picture-perfect village the Sims would live in. The surrounding areas were beautiful. We were a hop and a skip away from a lake and actual woods. As a family who had come from a house with a tiny balcony you could barely fit a flowerpot on and the 468 bus parking, with engine roaring, directly outside at any hour night or day, this was heaven. And it was a heaven I wanted for Esmé and the child I was going to have.

'You lot are brave, boy. I couldn't imagine having to go so far for things like plantain,' one friend sympathised when I told her that picking up things like black hair products or ingredients which were central to our Afro-Caribbean dishes were an utter ball-ache. Especially since I hadn't yet passed my driving test and the Milton Keynes bus service was about as dependable as a four-figure tax refund.

But it had felt worth it. As a mother all you want is to keep your babies safe and give them the best start, and deep down I felt that leaving London would help us do that.

And so, we settled in. Bode, ever the approachable one, made friends with our neighbours by stopping to chat. I kept my head down, using my ever-growing baby bump and frequent need to pee as an excuse not to get pulled into small talk (as you know by now, I'm not really great at small talk). The local high street offered the essentials we needed, apart from my beloved chicken spot Morley's, and a twenty-four-hour corner shop of some sort. And there was ample space at the local nursery, even though I was very aware that Esmé wasn't just the only black child present, but the only child of colour, period.

Soon enough, I had given birth to Richard Junior (named after his late grandfather), or RJ for short. As much as I once thought the name would be too heavy for him to bear, it was the one I actually liked. The birth itself was a 'gentle' elective C-section, which was performed on my thirtieth birthday. Looking at my new bundle of Pisces joy, I was overwhelmed with happiness, because we had stuck to our guns and avoided having to give birth to him at the same hospital in which I'd suffered such trauma with Esmé.

The newborn haze swallowed us whole, and although I'd secretly worried about being able to be there for both kids, who had such different needs, I need not have worried. I was enough. My new-found struggle was trying to perfect a home-life balance. By now I was establishing myself as an online content creator, and slowly but surely brands were starting to show an interest in the platform I was building. Ever since I had packed my publishing job in, this had always been the goal. That marketing role had given me insight into how steadfast content creators have to be in order to cultivate an audience who trust you. In between raising Esmé and baking cakes, it had been all I thought about and worked towards. By the time RJ was born, I had a very engaged and expansive social media following, and six weeks after his birth I met a wonderful team who would go on to help manage my career. All I had worked for had now begun to arrive right alongside my son.

We were no longer poor. And because I no longer had to think about making ends meet, I finally got the chance to enjoy motherhood. And I think it was bloody well deserved.

Before we knew it, Esmé turned four and it was time for her to start school. We had moved in time so that we had a good head-start in getting Esmé into our first choice of primary school, which was a twenty-minute walk away. There was a school a lot closer to our home, but we felt uncomfortable with the thought of her being the only black child in the school, like she had been in her nursery. Whilst we knew we had moved to an undiverse area, at least we had done so as a family. Day to day, I didn't want her to think she was completely alone, so I decided the one-mile trot would be worth it. We thought we had done our homework and we absolutely believed that we were not just going from the frying pan into the fire. It was always at the forefront of my mind that even though we were running from an ever-growing problem within inner-city London, we were alert to a different set of issues awaiting us now we had made the transition.

To my delight, although the population of her new school was overwhelmingly white, there were a few other black children – one of whom would be in her class.

'Well, at least she'll be able to interact with children who look like her,' Bode remarked on our way back from one of the settling-in days.

I agreed. It felt like, ever so slightly, a tiny weight had been lifted off my shoulders. Yes, we didn't live in the most diverse setting, but at least Esmé now had a few familiar faces she could glance upon if ever she felt confused and consumed by feelings of being the odd one out.

Aside from that she adored my niece, her cousin, who is a year and a half younger than her. My sister had become pregnant shortly after I had given birth to Esmé and giving birth had shocked her out of her dreamy social-media-induced haze and thrown her head-first into a world of adult responsibilities. She was no longer tardy and preoccupied, but focused on trying to give her daughter, my niece, all that she needed. It was nice to feel that whenever it seemed Esmé wasn't getting all she needed, I could call my sister and arrange for Esmé to spend some time in Brixton in the hope she'd find the same comfort I got from being surrounded by a culture and atmosphere that was created and maintained by black people.

But I was no fool. No intermittent cultural sabbaticals and late-night Amazon Prime purchases of books with black characters could make up for the fact that she was now one of so few and that it would, of course, start to creep into her mentality.

It started innocently enough.

I was making pancakes, so it must have been a Sunday, as that's pancake day in our house. In true Esmé fashion when she has something on her mind, she came into the kitchen and shuffled from foot to foot, like she was in desperate need of a pee.

'Esmé,' I said. 'What's up?'

'Mum, do you think we could cut my hair?' she asked, cocking her head to one side, observing me closely as if she was trying to find answers in my immediate reaction.

I kept my expression neutral, even though my soul was on fire. Without prying, I already knew that the root of this question was far deeper than the tiny hint she was now presenting to me. But I had to be delicate in my response, because I never wanted her to think that she couldn't express something to me without me judging.

'Well, we could cut your hair. I cut my hair all the time. But your locs are so beautiful, why would you want to do that?' I said carefully, setting down the mixing bowl of pancake batter and giving her my full attention.

'I don't know, it's just that some of the kids said that my hair isn't nice. They said it's really rough.' She shrugged.

The slow fire that began to burn in my chest now engulfed my entire body. I kneeled down to her level so I could look her in the eye.

'Now, you listen to me,' I began, desperately suppressing the rage in me. 'They are just jealous. Do you know how strong your hair is?' She shook her head at me. 'It's super strong. You can wear your hair up or down. You can wear it in a bun or bunches. You don't have to wash it every day and most importantly, you don't have a high chance of catching nits.' The last statement was me taking a dig at an imaginary person. The person who had made my daughter feel inadequate.

'What's nits?' she asked.

'Nits are insects that like to live on white people's hair,' I lied.

I knew good and well that anyone could get nits, but by

that point, I was too angry to care because I knew that this accusation had come from the mouth of a white child.

'Oh, that's gross!' She laughed, and, as always, her giggles immediately lifted my mood.

'Right? And that's something you never have to worry about,' I said, pulling her in for a hug, more so that she couldn't see the tears in my eyes than anything else.

'Mum, are the pancakes ready?' she asked, changing the subject with the same ease with which she had just shared what she would come to learn to be a microaggression.

'Yeah, lemon and sugar or maple syrup?' I asked.

Already I was starting to experience some of the things I'd feared when I had heard we were having a girl. Before I even held her in my arms, I'd thought about the many ways her confidence would be knocked and how everything from her name to her hairstyle was going to be an act of political defiance on my part.

Bode had said some years before, 'I'm really not sure about the locs thing, you know?'

Esmé's TWA (Teeny Weeny Afro) was getting out of control and I had zero canerow skills. I had sported a shaved head since I was seventeen and every woman in my family wore their hair free from chemicals intended to straighten their coils. I didn't want to impose a shaved head on such a young girl, but I didn't have the patience to learn how to canerow either, and so the most logical choice seemed to be forming her hair into locs.

'But what other choice do we have?' I replied. 'I don't want her to grow up thinking that she needs to chemically straighten her hair or be spending four hundred pounds on hair from Persia, or wherever the fuck it comes from.'

'I hear you, I hear you.' He laughed and let it go. He knew that there was no room for argument, as he often said that the fact I wore my natural hair was one of the reasons he had fallen in love with me. I would often jest that he just saw me as a cheap choice because if he had tried to date a woman who was into closures and frontals, he would forever be out of pocket. But all jokes aside, this isn't to say that I look down on black women who choose to flirt with false hair, but I do feel sorry for those who feel they have to depend on it or worse still, hide behind it. I had hoped that Esmé wouldn't struggle with the concept of her natural hair because her own mother, grandmother, great-grandmother and aunt all chose to celebrate their hair in its natural state. I've seen first-hand the friction that develops when a black woman who depends on wigs and weaves tries to encourage her own daughter to love her natural hair. The saying that 'children don't do as you say, but will do as you do', has never been more pertinent than when we are faced with the conundrum of dealing with black mothers and daughters and their choice in hairstyles.

And so Esmé was eighteen months old when my own mother greased her scalp and parted her hair before plaiting it into baby box braids, which would then allow it to form into locs (most people prefix that term with the word 'dread' but there is nothing dreadful about them, so we don't do that in our house). Even in that moment I understood how powerful this decision would be and I hoped that even when the choice would be tested and questioned, she would grow up to stand firm in the belief that the hair that grew from her head was beautiful, just as it was.

But now, running to school, my phone stuck to my ear, I would come to learn that it wasn't only Esmé's hair that her white classmates didn't find beautiful.

'Well,' continued her teacher, 'today at lunchtime, unfortunately, a young girl refused to play with Esmé because she said her skin was too dark.'

Even though I was sure I was moving forward towards the school, I felt as though I was being slowed down somehow, as if I were trying to run through water.

'Right, OK,' I replied, shocked at how matter-of-fact I sounded.

'Now, before you get too alarmed, I don't think the little girl meant any harm by it. I just think that these kids are at an age where they are starting to recognise differences. I did give her a five-minute time-out so she could think about her actions,' she went on. 'And unfortunately, I have had to write this up as a racist incident.'

'Five minutes?' I repeated. 'Right, got it, OK; thanks for letting me know.'

My head was spinning. Why was everything 'unfortunate'? And, more pressingly, why did it seem that the apologetic tone in her voice was being reserved for the fact that the white child who had ostracised Esmé had to be told off, more than for Esmé herself? And this had happened at lunchtime? Why was I only being called at the end of the day? Had they really left my daughter to stew in racist disregard since midday?

I was fucking livid. I already had visions of me running into the school like a black Miss Trunchbull. I would find the kid who'd insulted my child, pick her up by her undoubtedly blonde pigtails and throw her like a shot-put straight across the playground.

It was only when I ended the call that I realised I was crying. I automatically phoned Bode. It went to voicemail and I cut that call quickly, too. I had to speak to someone urgently. I needed someone to remind me that black people don't get to be angry even if the anger is righteous. Luckily, my friend Remi picked up on the first ring. Through tears, I recounted the teacher's call.

'Listen, sis, LISTEN,' said Remi, irate and clear. 'You have every right to go in there and turn over a table, but remember that when they catch us on CCTV, the evidence will always be used against us, never to support us. Do you hear me?'

I nodded, forgetting she couldn't see me.

'CANDICE!' she yelled. 'Do you HEAR me?'

'Yeah, yeah, I hear you.' I was now at the school gates.

'You're really powerful, Candice,' Remi continued. 'There is a way that this is going to have to be dealt with and you need to remember that your career and everything you've achieved means you're able to handle this in a way that white people fear most. And more to the point, you need to show Esmé the kind of stock she comes from. You ain't no regular degular. Hold space for your anger like Lil' Kim, but fuck them up like Michelle Obama.'

'Obama, got it,' I said. 'I'll call you back when I'm done.'

'Make sure, yeah,' and I heard the plea in her voice. 'Stay calm, Mama, stay calm.'

I'm not one of those mothers who gathers and socialises, as you know. It doesn't come naturally to me. I don't like playground gossip, forced friendships and I definitely have zero interest in WhatsApp groups with mothers just because we're in the same neighbourhood. Sure, I'll return a smile. I'll even wait for a woman with a pushchair to go first, but I'm not into the friend thing when it comes to pick-up time. I keep my head straight, collect my child and see it as a win if I can get in and out without interacting with anyone.

But today I slowed down and purposefully looked everyone in the eye, making sure my scowl was evident. Common sense would dictate that most of the parents I was throwing shade towards would be none the wiser about what had happened to Esmé that day, but common sense had been left behind wherever I'd picked up that call. All of a sudden, this entire environment was an enemy directly set up to target my child, and I was having none of it.

I barged my way through the gaggle of parents waiting outside Esmé's class. A staggered silence began to fall around me. I was being purposefully aggressive. I wanted someone to try me, anyone. But no one said a word.

'Esmé!' I bellowed, marching past her teacher. 'Esmé! Get up, let's get out of this place right now!'

'Mummy!' she shouted excitedly, but her expression changed when she could see how furious I was. 'Mum, what's wrong?'

'With me? Nothing. What's wrong is that your teacher called to let me know what happened to you today. She told me that a girl refused to play with you because you're black.' I was speaking very loudly, as I fixed Esmé's cardigan.

'Yeah,' Esmé replied. 'She said I was too dark.'

Watching her eyes fill with tears almost broke my heart. I took her hand. 'I'm so sorry this happened to you, Esmé. That little girl is racist, and I won't have that happen to you ever again.'

We walked towards the door, a wide and clear path already made for us by those who could see that something was amiss.

I looked at them all again with a deep contempt in my eyes. I kept one hand on Esmé's shoulder and the other balled into a tight fist, trying to remember what Remi had told me. We are never allowed to show uncontrollable anger. We are never allowed to flip a table. We are never allowed to retaliate violently. There was a way that this had to be dealt with and deep down I knew punching a parent square between the eyes was not the way.

'It's important to remember,' said Bode later that evening as we discussed what had happened, 'that the little girl would've heard this in her home.' I could already tell that he was trying to dilute my anger. It wasn't working.

I sucked my teeth. I had seen Michelle Obama twice that year as she promoted her book *Becoming*, so had heard first-hand how she'd dealt with similar blood-boiling experiences. I remembered how she'd encouraged everyone in the audience to 'go high, when they go low', but right now I was about as high as Mariah Carey's tolerance for being fully clothed.

'I hear that, but I'm just so fucking angry. I knew this would happen. I knew it.' I sighed, pinching the bridge of my nose and closing my eyes.

'I mean, I know you always tell me that I have so much to learn about being black and British,' said Bode. 'But honestly, after you called, I had to pull the car over and take a few moments out. I felt it for our baby, man.'

We'd been here before, of course, when we exchanged the seemingly never-ending differences between his experience of being raised as a part of the majority in Nigeria, and mine trying to grow up in a very different environment. And whilst I would never want my own child to go through pain, I admit that there was a minuscule part of me that felt like a point had been proved. For years I'd tried to illustrate to him how different it was for those of us whose blackness came with a side of the old Britannia. In our earlier days there were times when we barely spoke because he seemed to think black British people simply lacked self-belief. On countless occasions, he had made me feel like the stories I recounted where someone had made me feel less than because of the colour of my skin were childish fairy tales. There were times where he had made me feel like the microaggressions were in my head. And there were the few occasions where, whilst he didn't say it explicitly, I could tell he thought I had perhaps done myself no favours by coming across as aggressive.

But there was something to be said for the pain currently reflected in his eyes now. Here we had a young white girl, no older than five, who'd made it very clear that she didn't want to engage with our child precisely because she was black. There was no dismissive comeback for this one. It was racist through and through, and as Esmé's parents we had to think long and hard in regard to what we were going to do about it.

I had grown up like a gypsy. Moving as often as we did, the swift switch of postcodes often meant that I also had to change schools. Having spent my entire life feeling like I had no roots, I didn't want that for either of my children. But, in this case, our backs were against a wall. There was no way that I would allow Esmé to continue to be educated in a school who thought that a five-minute time-out was a sufficient punishment for racism, no matter what the age. I didn't once consider trying to work it out with the school because I was tired of explaining myself. There is a deep heaviness only the bones of black people who constantly have to highlight and explain racism feel. And please note I said black, not women or people of colour, because we don't share the same history.

As ever, it was like Bode was reading my mind.

'I guess all those notes you made about other schools will come in handy. She ain't going into Year One there,' he confirmed with a definite look in his eyes.

I exhaled. The silver lining was that she was only in reception, so thankfully I didn't feel too bad about pulling her out of the place.

I agreed. The only issue was that all the other schools I'd looked at were private. Now, when it comes to the arguments for and against private education, I've always been mindful of the person making the testimony to support their argument. Earlier that year I had spoken openly about looking into private education for Esmé and, to be honest, I may have had an easier time of it if I'd been discussing the state of my pubic hair. The Internet exploded. And there were two firm camps. The first was vehemently against it, suggesting that private education was a waste of money and at its heart no better than state education. The second were those who were all for it, even if their bank account meant that they couldn't yet provide that option for their child.

It was no surprise to me that even within this argument the two sides were distinguished by race. Unsurprisingly, black people were resoundingly in favour of private schools, many even sending me direct messages to disclose that's what they'd chosen for their kids. I think the fact that they didn't want to disclose this publicly helps illustrate the mood surrounding the conversation. To admit that you want to or do send your child to private school – especially in a social group that you can't be sure shares the same views – you have to be prepared to be somewhat of a pariah. So, as afore-mentioned, this wasn't shocking to me. Black people have always put a high price on education; so high, in fact, that most black people I know, specifically West Africans living in their home countries, were privately educated their entire school careers. My closest example of this was Bode, who had told me that private schooling was not 'a thing' amongst his friends and family. All his friends were privately educated, he had pointed out when I first tabled the idea of us doing the same for our children. He admits he now realises he grew up privileged, and within that privilege, they saw fee-paying schools as the standard.

Whilst this wasn't news to me, his casual attitude caught me off guard at first, and then I had to check myself. Why did I assume otherwise? Did I still subconsciously believe the narrative that most countries in Africa couldn't survive without aid from the Western world? Whatever the reason, it was beautiful to speak with a black man who saw what many would agree was one of the upmost privileges in the UK as accessible as fresh air. It was his nonchalance which really made me think we could do it. My career was on the up, and although my math skills weren't the greatest, I could see that with our combined earnings, the £3,500 per term a few of these schools were asking for wasn't that far outside of the monthly cost of full-time nursery in London (average £1,200 per month). When all was said and done, we had enough spare cash left to make this a possibility.

From my reading and research, talking to people and listening to my friends' kids' experiences, I knew that, typically, black children struggled to reach their full potential within the British state education system. Issues such as overcrowding, compounded with blatant racism from many educational professionals, usually added up to young black students either being ignored, written off as problematic or, at worst, excluded and sent to a pupil referral unit, perfectly preparing our children for the ever-feared and ever-present school-to-prison pipeline.

In my view, not only would a private school provide smaller classes and a wider choice of after-school activities, it would also teach Esmé to see herself as a leader. In my personal opinion, state education can encourage a worker-bee mindset: you arrive at this time, you listen, you go home; should you stray from the constructs we've provided we will have to punish you or, worse still, belittle your line of questioning and call you disruptive because you've dared to think in a manner which disrupts the status quo. My instinct told me that the private system could help Esmé flourish.

I once held a panel talk with two fabulous black women

at a private members' club. The conversation ranged from being self-employed to body image, but it was always rooted in being black. Afterwards, a black woman from the audience who I knew sent her daughters to private school came over to talk to me.

'That was amazing.' She smiled. 'I feel really inspired. But I hope you don't mind my frankness. I couldn't help but notice that your management team are all white? Why is that?'

I laughed. 'The same reason you send your daughters to private school,' I replied, looking at her dead in the eye.

'Now, you know as good as I,' I began, lowering my tone so only she could hear what I was saying, 'that if I wanted to hold a talk like this in a space as grand as this, that there would have to be a bunch of white women talking on my behalf. I don't like the way the system is set up, but it would be bad business to ignore it. Just like it would be bad business to not recognise that you're giving your black daughters a leg-up by educating them in a space which respects your money.'

I wasn't about to have anyone question the women who worked for and with me, no matter their race, but this seemed like the perfect moment to establish the fact that I understood we all had to play a good game to succeed.

She nodded. 'No, I understand, I understand. I meant nothing bad by it. And you're right, we know that money talks and, I mean, we both have little black girls. And we will do anything to give them the best, right?'

'Right,' I agreed, locking eyes with Bode and signalling for him to get me a much-needed drink.

Not today, Satan, I thought. Not today.

I use that conversation to help highlight what all black parents, specifically black mothers, know. If you want your child to succeed at school, you either have to be consistently present, often taking time away from your own work, or you have to pay for it. And by 'it', I mean an education that doesn't come with reports of your child being 'hyperactive' or 'disruptive' – because if black women have to fight the stereotype that they are perpetually angry, then our children definitely have to be wary about being marked as troublesome or hard of hearing, when a white child behaving the same way would be described as energetic or strong-willed. This situation was enough to remind me that if I wanted Esmé to have a fair educational experience, one where she could flourish, we would perhaps have to pay for it.

But before we moved forward with that, there were a few things I had to get off of my chest. I spent that night drafting up a borderline threatening letter to her head teacher. The situation had been handled appallingly. First and foremost, I was annoyed by the fact I wasn't alerted the minute the incident took place. Secondly, the fact that her teacher reserved her apologetic and defensive tone for the child who ostracised Esmé instantly confirmed my suspicions that she was being taught by a woman singing from the same prejudiced hymn book.

Finally, I was enraged that this girl's parents' identity was being protected. I was adamant that they caught a verbal smackdown from me, because a child of five doesn't just stumble across racism by themselves; that shit, that vile hate, is cultivated at home and I wanted a firm five minutes with the household bill payers.

Reading the letter back to myself, I smiled. I had always kept my line of work to myself, but the fact that I now had a CV rooted in diversity and inclusion helped me puff out my chest. It was important that even if Esmé was going to leave the school, that they understood they had to have better practices in place. But this isn't to say that some of the blame shouldn't lay with us.

'Make sure you quote their own school policy to them,' one friend mentioned in our group chat later that evening after I sent them a copy of my letter. I swallowed hard. I had never once read the school policy. Ever. I felt my face grow hot with shame. In a moment of madness, I admitted it.

'Don't worry,' she typed. 'Send it to me and I'll pull out the bits you want to throw back at them.'

Hastily I scoured the Internet for the policy. A few hours later she confirmed what I think we already knew: there was no mention of racial bullying in their school policy. There were no promises of safeguarding children of all races. There were no encouraging quotes about how their school would not tolerate anything but championing diversity and inclusion. It looked like the policy hadn't been updated since the Second

World War. And suddenly I felt very silly. If I had perhaps taken the time out to look at these things beforehand, then maybe I would've had more of a clue in regard to the kind of people I would be sending my child to school with.

Whilst I made note of our parental mistake, I didn't have time to meditate on it, as it was now more important than ever that the school understood where they were going wrong. I signed off the final draft by making it clear that Esmé would not be returning to school until we had a meeting with the head teacher scheduled, and made sure Bode knew to drop it off on his way into work the next day.

The school responded quickly, letting me know that they were more than willing to have a conversation, but they couldn't facilitate a conversation between ourselves and the aggressor's parents. I rolled my eyes.

'White people. White people-ing, innit?!' Bode shrugged when I recounted the phone call.

'Yeah, she's gonna defend this likkle yout to the end, mi cyan feel it.' Patois always became my default when I was vexed. We had been here numerous times before. A white person wrongs or offends and all their buddies gather around to offer their support in any way possible.

I did wonder if I was going to be able to make it through the meeting without losing my cool. Luckily Bode would be there, and if I felt myself losing my rag I would just pass the baton to him.

'Thank you so much for meeting with me,' Esmé's head

teacher said a few days later, gesturing to two empty seats for myself and Bode.

'No problem,' Bode said immediately, perhaps trying to ensure that I didn't just open my mouth and let it all fall out.

'This is Miss James, a teaching assistant whom I've asked to sit in on this meeting. I do hope you don't mind.'

Miss James extended her hand and I shook it firmly, narrowing my eyes as I tried to read her nervous expression.

'I'm so sorry we've had to meet under this circumstance,' the head teacher continued. 'And I appreciate that this has not been the best experience for Esmé.'

'Ah, I already have to stop you there,' I interjected. 'You call it an experience, her teacher called it an unfortunate incident. Where I come from, we call it racism. You must be able to call it what it is and not hide it behind words that make everyone except my daughter feel comfortable.'

I looked both the head teacher and assistant dead in the eye.

The seconds of silence that followed were vibrating with their discomfort. No one was going to get off lightly.

'Yes, do forgive me. The racist incident,' the head teacher confirmed. 'The issue is, given the age of the little girl who made the . . . racist comment and the fact that we're unable to facilitate a meeting between you and her parents, we do feel like our hands are tied.' She shrugged.

Bode sighed. I felt him already coming to the end of his tether.

'Look, Esmé isn't staying here,' he interjected. 'This is all new to me. I come from a place where I'm the majority and white people are the minority, so the fact I'm having to sit here and discuss the way my daughter was ostracised because she is black is not only heartbreaking but also a waste of our time. We are here because we want to know what is going to be done to ensure this does not happen again.' His full lips pressed together as if to suppress his anger.

'We understand, we do. Honestly, since all of this stuff with Brexit cropped up, we've had a rise in racism. With one family we even had to get Prevent involved because it was clear that the child was coming from a home who supported the National Front.' She sighed.

'Wow,' Bodé responded.

My eyes grew wide with fear. I had heard about Prevent before, but to think that a primary school had to use them because of fear of a child becoming radicalised, by way of those who believed that Britain should be occupied by whites only, really made me go cold, and was the final nail in the 'get Esmé out of this hellhole' coffin.

'It's a real struggle for us. You pointed out that our policy makes no mention of race or what happens when a racial incident like this happens and, to be honest, I didn't think it needed to. But I appreciate your suggestion and may have to now think otherwise.'

At that moment all of my anger went away. All of a sudden it was replaced by slight sadness. Looking past her role as head teacher and physical occupancy as a white woman, I could now see a woman in her early fifties who looked like she didn't know what to do, and I almost felt sorry for her.

'But you know, we are trying. I mean, next week we are having African drummers come in to try and teach the children about different cultures.'

'Shit,' I almost said. Instead, I snorted.

'African drummers? What even is that? Do you even know which country in Africa these drummers are from? Do you know what? Don't answer that. This is really bad. I appreciate you're trying, but African drummers aren't going to clear up the mess that's going on here.' I sighed, slumping back into my chair.

There was another moment's silence.

My head was spinning. From the perspective of being Esmé's mother, I was disgruntled and simply wanted to get my daughter out of this school as fast as I could. But now as I sat there as a black woman, listening to how little was happening to tackle what was a bigger problem than I had imagined, made my stomach curl in on itself. It was worse than I thought and now I wanted to remove her expeditiously.

'You're from Nigeria, aren't you, Mr Aboderin?' the head teacher questioned, turning her body to face him.

He nodded.

'So, don't you think it would be great for you to come in and teach Esmé's classmates all about where you're from?' She half-smiled.

I rolled my eyes.

If this wasn't Caucasity at its most premium, I don't know what was. Once again, black people had to simultaneously be the victim and the saviour. We had to take the brunt of the racism and also help others dismantle it. On one hand, Esmé's skin made her a target, and on the other, it made them want her dad to help point the arrow in a different direction. It was ludicrous.

Bode laughed. 'I'll see what I can do,' he lied.

The rest of the meeting was filled with tense pleasantries and a silent understanding that we were not best pleased and had no true intention of trying to dismantle the racism that was allowed to fester within the walls of the school. By the time we were back out onto the street, I was fit to explode.

'Fancy going to the crêpe spot? You look like you could do with a G&T,' Bode remarked, pulling me close.

'Yeah, we've got time to kill,' I agreed.

Over a firm Hendricks for myself and a hot crêpe for Bode, we tried to make sense of what we had just heard.

'Bruv, Prevent, you know?!' I cried rhetorically between gulps of my drink. 'I'm telling you, if they had to use Prevent to help a child not become radicalised by Islam, the entire school would know about it, but because this version of terrorism doesn't support the narrative that black and brown people are the problem, they've kept it under wraps.' I sighed, shaking my head with disbelief.

'Listen, let's just focus on what we have to do to make Esmé feel supported. There are only a few months left until the end of the year. I think it's time we go through those prospectuses you've been saving.' He winked.

Shit, I was busted. But this had always been the way I operate. Since we had moved into the area, every so often I'd pick up a prospectus for yet another school I knew good and well we couldn't afford, but I kept them anyway in the hope that one day we would just go for it. And even though our hands were forced and I'm pretty sure my bank account would suffer organ failure, it was time to jump out of the boat. We both knew I already had my eye on three schools in particular, but there was one which, mainly due to the fact that their website and prospectus showed such a diverse range of children, meant that they were in the lead by far. Once we were home later that evening, I sent an email enquiring about attending an upcoming open day.

'Wow, Mum, this looks like a palace!' Esmé remarked as our car slowly made its way up a gravelled driveway that gave way to a building so big, it felt as though my eyes went crossed trying to take in all its magnificence at once.

'Mate, it looks like . . .'

'Hogwarts!' Bode and I said in unison, both giggling uneasily.

The school was no more than a fifteen-minute drive away from our home, but it looked so grand it may as well have been in another country. Surrounded by miles and miles of open fields and tucked well away from the traffic-filled A5, it felt both intimate and welcoming.

Glancing quickly at Bode I could tell he felt out of his depth, which comforted me immediately, because if there was one stereotype I lived up to, it was the one that says black people can't swim. We were both drowning, but it was in our best interests not to show it.

'Wow, this is amazing!' Esmé gasped as she stepped out of the car.

'It is, it is!' I responded, watching her skip ahead.

The doors to the school stood pronounced like two grey giants, giving way to a dark wood interior. Inviting Chesterfield sofas were dotted around the entranceway, and nearby there was a grand glass cabinet which held trophies for things like rugby and chess.

I at once recognised the woman before us as the head teacher. Our most recent lesson still slightly stinging, I had studied the school's prospectus in-depth, being sure to take note of not only their policies with regards to racism, but also all the teachers' faces. A short, firm woman with a hairstyle similar to Anna Wintour's bob, she seemed kind but very no-nonsense. Right up my street.

'Hello, Esmé!' she sang. It was clear that I wasn't the only one who had done my research.

'Wait! How did you know my name?' Esmé gasped, looking back at us with wide eyes.

'Well, I am the headmistress and I must know all the comings and goings. If not, how would I keep you all safe?'

'Good point!' Esmé confirmed.

We were shown into a hall so majestic I half expected to see the flash of a wizard's cloak and a sorting hat. Instead, it was filled with a group of parents who looked equally out of their depth. They clung to their cups of coffee and saucers piled with Victoria sponge as if they were on the last few dinghies allotted during the sinking of the Titanic.

I swept my eyes over the room and kept a smile plastered on my face. Bode always excelled in situations like this. He was a natural smooth-talker and he refined those skills in his day job. I, on the other hand, worked and excelled best when I was alone, and that didn't bode well when it came to these kinds of group activities.

A more junior but stricter-looking member of staff appeared and introduced herself as the head of the junior school.

'The plan today is to let you get a feel for the school and ensure that your little ones feel as though you will be making the right choice for them. Other members of staff, some students and I will walk you around in small groups and answer any questions you may have. After that we will reconvene here and talk about the next steps.' She smiled.

'That's the part where they make us sell our kidneys,' Bode whispered in my ear.

I tried to stifle my giggle. But he was right. I understood that this was still a business and today was a bit of show and tell. Of course, they would use the most glowing and dependable of students to show us around. Of course, everything would be polished to a high shine; I wasn't that slow. Today I would have to depend on my intuition. As a parent, I had come to depend on that slight tug that lingered beneath my belly button and it had never failed me unless I decided not to listen to it. I wouldn't make that mistake again.

Over the next ninety or so minutes we were taken from room to room, where various teachers were waiting, ready to repeat their rehearsed speech in regard to what they would be teaching our children. Whilst they rambled on, I took in the plentiful displays which showed not just the children's schoolwork but also pictures of current students. I was happy to see that there seemed to be more black children present in this school than at Esmé's last. In some instances, there were names of the children present below each picture. Every one of their last names was Nigerian. Go figure.

When we arrived at their library, I let the voices of the other parents become white noise as I flicked through their offerings. The range of books on offer was diverse and inclusive, with even titles in French and German. OK, they weren't doing too badly.

But I think what sold it for me was seeing Esmé go from room to room and being beside herself with all that could be provided to support her education.

'Mum, look – a whole kitchen!' she exclaimed when we were shown into the food technology space.

'Woah! Look at those drums!' she squealed once we were in the music room.

'Oh my gosh, all of this space for meeeeeee!' she yelled, charging into the on-site 'forest school' with her young chaperone, a slight seven-year-old who spoke English, German and French and who was moving to Sweden the following year.

No matter where you come from or what race you are, there isn't a mother on the face of the earth who doesn't want to give their child the best. And seeing Esmé's reaction to the school really made me think perhaps this was Hogwarts after all, because I was going to have to pull a rabbit out of a hat to make this happen no matter what.

'So, I'll leave the paperwork over there and if you have any questions, don't hesitate to come and talk to me,' the head of juniors advised later on.

'What you thinking?' I asked Bode, reaching out to take RJ from him. Thankfully, at fourteen months old, he was a joy to take out. Although he had found his feet, he wasn't yet confident enough to start demolishing the place.

He folded his arms.

'I think it's great. Just look at her,' he said, gesturing with his chin to where Esmé was playing. 'The curriculum seems broad and I did spot a very positive piece of artwork on the walk around,' he went on.

I had noticed it too: a painting of various portraits of brown faces drawn next to white ones. Some with bindis, others with headscarves, a few with glasses, all smiling and beneath it, one line: 'All children are welcome here.'

I nodded.

In place of the fear that once occupied Bode's eyes was now just solid determination. Even though he was a salesman by trade and knew all the tricks in the book, he had fallen hook, line and sinker for the school.

Looking around the room, it was clear to see that other couples were having this same conversation. Sure, most of them had pulled up driving vehicles with the newest number plates and many of them wore watches with five-figure price tags, but I knew more than anyone that it meant very little. Deciding to give your child private education usually came with a massive sacrifice and the nail-biting worry of being able to pay the fees each term. And it wasn't just the fees. Speaking with women whose children I knew who had attended private school, they let me know that the fees were just the start. What about uniform and extracurricular activities? Those were also necessities, and it would all add up quite quickly.

I shoved my fears aside. I had been here before and if it wasn't for my grandad's wise words, I perhaps never would have met Esmé's glowing face. As ever, we would jump first and pray the parachute would open later.

'All OK?' the headmistress asked as I went to pour myself a cup of coffee.

I smiled.

'Very well, thank you. The tour was brilliant. Thank you to you and your staff for putting our minds at ease.'

'No worries at all, that's what we are here for. I know it can feel overwhelming, but please take your time in deciding. We aren't going anywhere.' She grinned, before going off to chat with other parents.

She was right; they weren't going anywhere, but Esmé was. She was moving from a space I knew to a place I'd never been before. Space usually withheld for only the terribly rich and privileged. And, although it worried me slightly, I was more excited than anything else. I was about to give my baby girl the world, and Jesus, I think she deserved it.

9

SMALL AXE, BIG TREE

*In December 2018, Amnesty International released
a report of their research into online abuse
which found that black women were amongst
the most abused groups on social media.*

Like many new mothers I know, I clung to the Internet like
a newborn suckling on its mother's breast. Pregnancy had
already taught me that if I depended on traditional media to
help me see a version of motherhood and parenting, which
not only included but reflected me, I'd have to wait a while.
To put it in context, the first time I saw a black woman on
the cover of a parenting magazine was in 2018, on a news-
stand outside the Paris Metro – a whole five years after I'd
given birth to Esmé.

One platform I'd used more than most was Instagram.
Sure, I'd frolicked with Mumsnet if Esmé was unwell or
if I was worried about the speed of her development. But

to be honest, I couldn't get my head around the way the site worked. Things like threads and all the acronyms really grated on me, so Instagram was where it was at for me. I liked the simplicity of it. Like any proud parent, I uploaded videos and pictures of Esmé, more for myself than anyone else. But as I began to explore the pictures that were hashtagged with phrases like 'real parenting' and 'welcome to motherhood', it dawned on me that just like in traditional media, there didn't seem to be much diversity when it came to the way motherhood was presented on social media either.

I wanted to change that. Still, who was I? I was just a very young black woman annoyed with the fact that I struggled to see myself represented. I knew that there were a multitude of layers as to why that was and how difficult it was going to be to change that.

First and foremost, the black community is very guarded. If you've come this far in the book and you aren't black, you will perhaps be thinking, really? You seem pretty open to me. But let it be known that I am a rarity. Most of the black community ain't sharing shit. From their mac and cheese recipes to how we stop our black from cracking, it's all under lock and key. And who could blame us? The things we have suffered in our textured history have encouraged us to put up barriers in the hope that, in keeping ourselves to ourselves, no other race would ever again be able to sell us into slavery. Exhibiting our private lives on social media wasn't something that was yet seen as normal.

And so, I continued to do me, as I always have. I understood that me sharing the more intimate details of my life on social media might raise a few eyebrows with the aunties who still believed that children should be 'seen and not heard', but living for the aunties don't get you very far. I made a silent promise that if I got the chance to change the narrative, I would.

By the time Esmé was coming up to two years old, I was working in the marketing department for a well-known publisher. I was working full-time, leaving the house at 6.45am and, on days when the South Western trains were agreeable, I could perhaps be back home by 6.45pm. As the months went on, I began to find the balance impossible. Watching the clock, running out of the office like a crazed banshee, feeling overcome with guilt when Esmé was sick and trying to take into consideration that my own mother, who looked after Esmé whilst I was at work, was suffering from ill health herself. So, after a lot of private deliberation, I decided to step back from my job, much to the blood-boiling anger of Bode.

But it hadn't been a waste of time, far from it. The bulk of my time at work had been spent trying to get hold of bloggers (the word 'influencer' wasn't yet in vogue) in an attempt to get them to promote an upcoming or backlist title (publishing talk for 'old books'), so we could access a new readership. In the six months I'd been doing this, I'd noticed two things: I was never once given the details of a black blogger, and the going rate for advertising our books on their sites and forums was often more than I made in a week. Those two things ground my gears no end.

In fact, despite extensive research, it was a struggle to find the handful of popular black British content creators that did exist. And even upon finding them I had to ask myself, why weren't these women being presented with the same opportunities? Why were they never on the contact sheet? And why on earth did no one see this as a problem? It was all business, I was pragmatic enough to understand, but it still left my tongue soured, because what that truly meant was that black women were once again not being given the space they needed to excel, which then equated to them either being paid unfairly or not at all.

Remaining in that pragmatic frame of my mind, I couldn't help but recognise what a winner of a business opportunity this could potentially be for me. With advertising on social media still in its infancy, my instinct told me that this was about to become an open market. And if I played my cards and content right, this could be the answer to my flexible-working prayers. I didn't need to take a class in business to understand that businesses make money when there is a gap in the market they can fill. There was a black-woman-shaped hole with my name on it, that much was clear. It was time to make my private thoughts public.

'Right,' Bode fumed as I explained I was going to set up a blog and become a 'content creator'. 'So, you mean to tell me you're going to leave a job which actually pays and has helped take some of the financial strain off of this household, to be a YouTuber?'

I sighed. It did sound crazy when he put it like that. 'We both know this roundabout isn't working. I feel stressed and like I never get to see Esmé at all. And I have an idea about how I might be able to build a brand and be in a position where I can dictate when I work and when I don't. You just have to trust me.'

And whilst he was against the idea with every fibre of his being, he did agree that the stress of trying to keep Esmé cared for whilst we both went out to work was proving harder than we both expected. Yes, without my salary, we would be back on the breadline, but my instinct told me it was now or never. I'd watched for so long now as white mothers took a monopoly of a market that had changed their lives insurmountably. Was it unfair for me to want that same kind of control over my own time and the financial liberation it brought? Fuck no. I wasn't going to talk myself out of a good thing. I was tired of not being able to see women who looked like me in the parenting space. So, come what may, I was determined to walk off the plank into cyberspace.

As we so often hear about these magical social-media unicorns who go viral overnight and wake up with a million followers, I want to make it absolutely clear that I had no such luck. I knew that I'd need a substantial following in order for anyone to take my cries for diversity and inclusion seriously, but I also wasn't willing to create content that didn't truly resonate with my community. Being labelled as a sell-out is second only to being called a snitch, and it was a peculiar balance to strike. For example, I didn't want to portray the black community as constantly struggling.

By now, I hope you know what I mean, but for clarity, I didn't want to be complicit in pushing false stereotypes of black women living in high-rise concrete blocks waiting on a giro cheque, shouting at one of our many 'fatherless' children. We also aren't all drug dealers only interested in lacing our kids in designer gear. Like every other race on earth, we are varied and nuanced and we were long overdue to see a more balanced representation of ourselves. I felt it was my duty to remind people that black people weren't just surviving, but also thriving. Since I often struggled to see images of completely black nuclear families – I'll tell you for free that any advertising using interracial couples is not the same thing, it's a marketing ploy to appear diverse whilst not pissing off their white audience – I made an exaggerated point of sharing pictures of our family unit. Here we were, a very black mum and dad raising a very black child. Slowly, a community who appreciated what we were trying to promote began to gather. But this certainly didn't happen overnight. It took years before I grew a substantial social-media following.

With the positive comments came the negative. I could easily look past the fact that some of my biggest detractors or naysayers in the earlier days were black women. These women were very much FUBU-minded – For Us By Us – and for the life of them they couldn't understand why it seemed like I wanted to be so badly accepted by the white mummy set. Whilst the sneak disses stung, I could see where they were coming from; but I was adamant that we black people have always known that the way we were treated was unfair. Our culture and societal contributions are usually stolen and repackaged (baby carrying, anyone? African elders visibly laugh at the price of these Ergobaby contraptions. We've been doing that with two pieces of spare material way before any baby magazine said this way of carrying babies was in fashion) to suit an audience we are excluded from and therefore do not profit from. I wanted a family like mine to be front and centre of it all, visible and present, because I believe you can't be what you can't see. And only by forcing myself into a space that wasn't supposed to be mine would true change be made.

To help illustrate this, I always use my KFC-table analogy (NB: not the same as the pyramid analogy). On one table there is a KFC bucket. Crammed around the table are black women, who are expected to share this one KFC bucket, because that's what society likes to say we are deserving of – not just the measly amount to be split amongst so many women, but also the fact that it's chicken. At another table, there's a banquet of free-range organic chicken. Hell, there is more than chicken, there is avocado and quinoa too (both personal favourites of mine). There is so much food laid out for those sitting at this table that the white women around it don't know what to do with it. But the black and the white women never switch tables.

Now, the interesting thing is that no one ever publicly said we couldn't switch tables. Whilst I enjoy the comfort that KFC brings, black women deserve to be able to have a choice. And so, in creating my blog and using Instagram to share snippets of my life, I made the choice to take my chair from the KFC table and plonk it with the others at the organic one, determined to stay no matter whom it made uncomfortable. And you better believe it made some people twitch, but more on that later.

As time went on and my online community grew, I was able to have more forthright conversations about how beige the parenting landscape was. And then one day, off the back of a negative Mumsnet thread that was discussing the biggest parenting bloggers in the UK, a light bulb appeared. I'd noticed that, yet again, not one of the bloggers discussed was a woman of colour.

'I couldn't care less about the actual thread,' I ranted into my phone on my Instagram Stories. 'All that I can see is that white and middle-class parenting still seems to be all that is on offer. Don't they think it's time they make motherhood more diverse?' This was the first time I had ever confronted what had grated me for so long head on. I had danced around the glaringly obvious previously, but now I jumped head-first into the fire.

I clearly struck a nerve. Other women who agreed that

change was needed got in contact, and we decided to pull together and create an Internet space which was more reflective of the parenting world we knew to exist. It would be called Make Motherhood Diverse and we would call on all kinds of mothers and parents to make submissions. Using Humans Of New York – the already popular Instagram profile which shares images of seemingly everyday people and uses the caption to share an interesting titbit of their life – as our template, we put our heads down and launched the platform in the autumn of 2017 to much acclaim.

It was like we'd created an oasis in a desert. Word spread quickly that there was a place you could go to feel like your version of motherhood was represented. It was a revelation to me as I read the posts women were kind enough to share and the caring responses of others engaging with the space. It made me realise that I wasn't the only one who felt as though I'd been cut out of this universal narrative of motherhood. It became clear to me that I'd only ever been searching for myself but that as a black woman, I wasn't, by a long way, the only one who had been ignored or made to feel invisible.

Make Motherhood Diverse soon showed me how selfish and tunnel-visioned I'd been.

Where were the Asian mums?

Where were the disabled mums?

Where were the mums in same-sex relationships?

Early in 2018, I found myself at the centre of a shitstorm. An image was circulating online. And in that image were five or so white women announcing that they would be the judges of a competition which was backed by both a well-known brand and magazine, called *Star Mum*. Of course, all of the judges were white. There wasn't even a mixed-raced woman present to make it look like someone had tried.

My direct messages buzzed. 'Have you seen this absolute whitewash of a campaign?' the first read. 'As part of Make Motherhood Diverse, you have to say something.' It went on, and soon hundreds of similar messages began to swing my way.

My stomach flipped like I was on a fairground ride. The problem for me went beyond the already problematic image, as I recognised one of the women in the picture and I didn't want it to seem as though I was attacking her personally. At the same time, I couldn't ignore how tone-deaf and lazy this was and how it went against everything I and Make Motherhood Diverse were fighting for. So, after hours of deliberation, I decided to say something. Running my words by anyone I knew before finally uploading my post to Instagram, I challenged this narrative and thought that would be the end of it.

'Listen, it's not about being controversial, it's about being inclusive. I take nothing away from the women in the photo, but if we don't continually send up red flags when the idea that motherhood is only for the white and middle class is promoted, then we have a problem. It's not like me to debate sharing something, but as I see the DMs rolling in it would be wrong of me to champion something like Make Motherhood

Diverse and not call it like I see it. I know too many mothers who already don't seek the friendship and support they need in the early days because they feel excluded from the local baby group. As big-ass pregnant as I am, I won't ever not sing for those who feel they have been silenced. Do better [redacted].'

Even reading that back now, in no way do I see that as fighting talk, but many would read it as otherwise.

Unbeknown to me, I was about to lose my Internet scandal virginity, and what unravelled after that post was a month of hell. Other Instagram users saw it as a perfect moment to draw a battle line between myself and one of the women in the post, as she was the one that was considered a blogger rather than a celebrity. There were even some black women going public to say they supported her decision to agree to be a judge in the competition wholeheartedly, and telling others not to pay any attention to what I was saying as I was clearly getting a little above my station.

I had been sucked straight into the call-out culture vortex.

People assumed I wanted attention and a quick way to grow my social-media following, but they were wrong. I just wanted businesses to see that they couldn't keep excluding so many of us out there. Mothers of all kinds are consumers of a plethora of brands that continuously cut them out of their advertising, fully expecting them to stay silent, whilst forever lining their pockets. This moment – albeit small and insignificant in comparison to the real world – was a massive online wake-up call to those who were lazy and excluding in their casting, even if they didn't mean to be.

To be honest, when I pointed out how that image was lacking in diversity, I didn't expect the noise that followed. I was, and in many ways still am, an Internet nobody. I knew that there were many who thought I had some cheek bringing attention to this issue, even if it was the right thing to do. But for every person who perhaps believed that I should have kept my mouth shut, there seemed to be five more who were very supportive of the fact that I stuck my neck above the parapet. Lots of people saw the clear wrongdoing in regard to what was happening, but for a number of reasons many didn't want to be the one to say anything. And I understand that completely, because I was shit-scared before speaking up. I was trying to build a career in media, and this had the potential to blow everything to smithereens before I had even started to achieve all I had dreamt about. But sometimes, the truth is worth it.

The next couple of days were very loud. Many people just wanted a cat fight. It would be a couple of years later until I spoke with the other blogger in the picture. She had been sent death threats and images of the Ku Klux Klan. Many had incorrectly painted her as a racist when in fact she had made a mistake that I think we are all guilty of. Including myself.

And this mistake is not looking for anyone except yourself.

Yes, I've made that mistake before. Like I said, before the launch of Make Motherhood Diverse, I was only ever looking out for myself as an underrepresented woman. I hadn't even thought about the others amongst us. So, I do understand how easy it might be as a white person to not even clock that anything or anyone was missing. But what I was absolutely adamant about was that we needed to be calling attention to situations like these in the name of change. If it was a simple matter of oversight that the organisers were willing to make right, then that was one thing. But if they weren't, then that was a whole different scenario and one that Make Motherhood Diverse and I would be there to challenge.

But change itself is exactly that: a challenge. I now had to deal with the fact that I had many more eyes on me, and with that comes many opinions – and most of them not very kind.

My fingers had been e-burned, and I quickly realised that I never wanted to be part of the call-out culture again. I guess it didn't help that I was pregnant at the time, but even though I knew in my gut that pointing out the issues with that campaign would do a lot of good in the long run, in real-time it felt like a huge mistake. I didn't want Internet notoriety because I apparently came for one of the UK's biggest mummy bloggers. I wanted brands and business to sit up and take notice of all mothers, not just the ones they could see themselves in. And even though I stand by the fact that I only wanted to see a change for the better, I quickly got hip to the fact that I couldn't control what others thought of me.

In that regard, I learned that there are other impactful ways to get a message across, and so I kept my head down and at every chance I got tried to make sure that brands and businesses I worked with weren't being tokenistic. When certain jobs came my way, I asked my management to request a call sheet so I could be sure that I wasn't the only black face on set. I opened up my inbox to women who wanted to know how they could also get to work at making sure the spaces they occupied represented the world in which they lived. As uncomfortable as it is, I'm always the first to flag when there needs to be a shift behind the camera, too. If the PR team behind these campaigns reflects only a small portion of society, then that was a problem.

Lastly, wherever I could, I made sure that not only were other black and brown women cast in ads and campaigns, but that they were getting paid to be there, too. The Internet consistently reminded me how easy it was to think that calling something out or posting, sharing or retweeting could actually contribute to change. It doesn't. It's about the questions that are asked and things that are done when no one is looking, when there are no likes to receive and the high likelihood is you won't even get a thank you.

As my personal brand grew, so did the opportunities to interact with the very women who had for so long been regarded as the cream of the crop of the online motherhood space. Whilst I can't attest to being friends with any of them, we were now colleagues, often coming across each other in both online and real-life spaces, and I had hoped that we could all learn that only good could come from allowing a more diverse and inclusive group of women to sit at this table.

But, as the young folk would say, never, ever get lost in the sauce.

If you have been following me on social media, you will know that the back end of 2019 was particularly interesting, to say the least. The queen bee of UK mummy blogging, who was also an NHS midwife, admitted to being a troll on one of the UK's most vitriol-filled 'forums'.

I had word about this a few days before the news went public and, as naive as ever, I just thought, 'Oh shit, sucks to be her, I guess,' and promptly went back to focusing on my writing. But as the days went on, everything became more peculiar, and once again I found myself at the centre of a shitstorm.

'She is very aggressive,' she wrote about me on this gossip site in February of 2019. 'She brings everything back to race, class and privilege because she knows it will silence people. She uses race as a weapon.'

Now, let me stretch before I continue writing, as this is the first time I've discussed this situation on my terms. What she wrote chilled me to the core – not least because, as I previously mentioned, this was my worst nightmare. In August of 2019, I recorded a podcast episode with her. Her podcast was all about sharing birth stories, so I reiterated in detail what had happened to me when I gave birth to Esmé, and urged people to sign the petition to try to get the government to investigate why black women in the UK are five times more likely to die in childbirth. I am no fool, so I won't pretend that we were besties braiding each other's hair, but I play with an open hand. If I had known what she really had thought about me, I would never have offered her a fart, to be frank. To have aligned myself so publicly with someone I thought to be an ally, who then turned out to say I used my race as a weapon, was like being stabbed in the back.

Whilst this woman was never a friend, we were often in the same spaces – a bit like how you find yourself playing politely with acquaintances in the office you never spent time with outside of that space. Now that this had been revealed, something in my subconscious prickled. Was I really that surprised by her actions? Absolutely not. Earlier that same year, my mother and I had attended an event she was hosting, and I can't even remember what I was talking about, but she leaned in towards me and my mother to let me know that 'It's not the Candice show', with a soured undertone as if I'd pissed her off. As soon as we left, my mother warned me that she had no good intentions for me and that I needed to be careful. I love my mum, I really do, but sometimes I think she lets the juju go to her head. In this instance I have to say she was a perfect judge of character, because this event was in March 2019; a month after she had already written about me on that forum.

The story becomes even more Shakespearian, as a few weeks before this became public knowledge, she'd invited me to her jewellery launch. As I left, she hugged me very tightly and thanked me for being on her podcast, even claiming it was 'the most downloaded' episode. Whilst, on one hand, the deceit makes my stomach flip, on the other, she unwittingly handed me the sweetest gift, by becoming the very embodiment of all that I ever said black women have to deal with on- and offline.

When it all came out, as much as I wanted to defend myself, I knew that uttering even a single word would play into the aggressive narrative she had laid out for me. Even in a moment of well-earned fury, I still had to play a game. I couldn't just go online and say what I thought of her. And she knew it. People like that always know that using words like 'aggressive' and 'angry' when speaking about black women silences us before we have even had a chance to defend ourselves. Me sending for her could have potentially soured my brand and blown up all I had worked for. There was no way in hell I was going to give her that satisfaction. And as someone once told me, 'Silence can never be misquoted.' So, I knew I would have to remain silent until I felt it was the right time to speak.

Whilst I'm on the subject, it's important to remember she is not alone in this. Years before this, I had been in a video on YouTube where unfortunately the comments were not moderated. The racism was so acute, I lay in bed for a week crying. Every other comment used the word 'nigger'. Sometimes the troll would get creative and call me 'God damn ugly nigger' and others would say 'Who allowed this monkey to speak?'. So, although her comments were tamer, I had felt this pinch before. And the reality is that any black woman who is bold enough to have an online presence has more than likely experienced the same thing. The only difference with this woman is that she got caught.

I have to give my fellow black sisters their props, as many of them had been right all along. As much as I had elbowed my way into this industry to try and make way for other women that look like me, one woman's actions have made it clear that most already occupying this space saw me as nothing more than an annoyance. Of course, they would never admit this publicly, especially since their mate was now being branded as a racist. But at my end the damage had been done, and now my eyes were forever opened.

I can't lie to you all. I wish there was an eloquent way to say this, but this shit is fucked. Utilising the Internet to try and build a brand or business whilst cuddling up to women who wouldn't know how to spell sisterhood or ally if their lives depended on it is a very dangerous place to find yourself in. Not just because of how suspicious and untrusting it makes you, but because it has a detrimental effect on your mental health. Once again, I'd been targeted for something I can't and wouldn't change. It has taken a massive toll on me.

Considering how much this has all cost me personally, I think people would be surprised to know that I wouldn't change a thing. A dear friend of mine, who is also a tarot reader, once introduced me to 'maktoob', an Arabic word meaning 'it is already written', and that is how I feel about all of this. It was never ever going to play out another way. If I have to be used as a tool to uncover the real thinking of women that dominate this space, I will fall on my own sword, time and time again, if that's what it takes to prove that there is still so much work to do.

Because here is the fucking gag.

Social media is very reflective of the world we live in. And some women like those mentioned above do not shrug off their judgements or racist ideologies before they go out into the world. They carry these violent stereotypes with them and weaponise them against black women in every facet of our lives, including motherhood.

But this doesn't mean that there is no hope. Just as it felt like all the great work that communities like Make Motherhood Diverse were doing was being overruled by a wave of gossip and negativity, I was able to share some images that were taken for the app Peanut. Having been hired to consult on the photo shoot to make sure that we were representing as many mothers as possible, the reaction to the pictures came like some much-needed gas in my tank. There were people who truly understood what I was trying to do. And that was my light in the darkness.

And during the editing process of this book, something very humbling happened. One of the first ever women to really champion Make Motherhood Diverse, who gave us a very detailed insight into how she lived with a chronic illness, passed away. Rachel, or BreathlesslyMothering as she was known online, was one of the models for the Peanut photo shoot. News of her inevitable (she had made it clear in a New Year post that it was the start of a decade she surely wouldn't see the end of due to her ill health) and yet untimely passing sent shockwaves through our online community. She was a real one. Always showing love and support and in turn getting it straight back. Women like Rachel remind me why it's important to keep showing up even when ninety per cent of the time it's going to feel like hell. You have to be in it for the ten per cent. Because the ten per cent are the little glimpses of togetherness, hope, joy and progression. It's so fleeting, but that ten per cent cuts through darkness all the same. Just like Rachel's life did.

I think what I went through in real life and online has made a book like this all the more necessary. Hopefully it will start to help humanise the black British motherhood experience, which, let's face it, before this was always narrated by someone who had never lived it. It's why titles like 'Baby Mother' are still thrown around as an insult. It's why people are still shocked to see young black families sticking together. It is also why trying to get people on board with the idea that black women's lives are just as – if not, dare I say, more – important than reducing our use of plastic, is so damn difficult.

But here I am.

And here I will be.

Long after the dust has settled and apps like Instagram are as archaic as MySpace, this fight will still be ongoing. I'm only really interested in engaging with those who have taken on the themes within this book, who have not only been entertained but also enlightened, and who are now impassioned to see how they can actively help make a change and not just be seen to be doing so.

What will you do when nobody is watching?

That really is the question.

And, because I like all things to come full circle, I shall end how I began.

I may have a baby.

I may be a mother.

But I am not your baby mother.

ACKNOWLEDGEMENTS

Father God, thank you for being a lamp onto my feet even when I refused to see the light. All the thanks and praise would still not be enough.

To my ancestors – I see you and I thank you.

To myself, thank you for believing in you, Candice. A friend recently asked, 'What would Candice, living on Kellett Road, eating at Speedy Noodle, have to say to Candice today?' I paused and then said, 'She would walk past me, as she wouldn't be able to recognise me.' That is a full-circle moment which you are deserving of thanking yourself for.

To my children, there would be no 'this' if not for you. When the day comes that I'm no longer able to remind you that you should never take 'no' for an answer and you can do anything, I hope this book serves as a reminder. Take it all, my loves. You deserve it.

Papa B, the epitome of ride-or-die. Thank you for giving

me space to become the woman I am today and being a brilliant father to our children.

Thank you to my mother.

To my nan and grandad, thank you for taking me on as if I were your firstborn. Thank you for both turning your backs on coconuts and ocean breeze to come to a country that has not always been kind. You both made a move for those you had not yet met and I am now benefiting from the hard times you experienced, for which I am always grateful..

To my sister and brother, thank you for supporting me always.

To my niece, Mimi, thank you for being a ray of sunshine.

To my uncle P, the man with nine lives! You are the embodiment of positive reincarnation. Thank you for showing me that it's not over until it's over and until then, there is always time to try again.

To my extended family, and most notably my father-in-law, Olutunde Oyegoke Aboderin, who answered all of my questions pertaining to the Yoruba culture, thank you.

To Charlie Dark, thank you for being the father figure that I didn't always want but God knew I would need. Continue to inspire.

To all of my IRL friends including but not limited to Remi, Mahlon, Sham Sham, Emma, Leona and Jess. Thank you so much for putting up with me and inspiring me during the creating of this book.

Krishna, Krish, KK. You were the first friend to show me what unconditional friendship looks like. Before social media and words like 'gender fluidity', you presented yourself in a way which made me question everything. You were – no, you still are – one of a kind. RIP.

To everyone at Found Entertainment – quite possibly the best management team in the UK. But with special thanks reserved for Francesca Zampi, Harry Grenville and Daisy Janes. You all have moved heaven and earth for me and I won't forget it.

Thank you to the entire Quercus team, especially Bethan Ferguson who saw something special in this book from the early days, and then of course my cool, calm and collected editor Katy Follain who has trusted that I know what I'm talking about and has given me the space needed to produce a work like this.

And to you, yes, you!

No matter how this book has found you, you have endured it for this long and I am very grateful to your commitment to my work. To those of you who support me online, please never underestimate how powerful that support is in my real, day-to-day life. It's a pleasure to communicate with you.

And last but by no means least, to my father, Richard. I have felt your hand upon my shoulder in the darkest and coldest of moments and there are no words to correctly evoke how much I would have loved to share this moment with you in the physical. But I have no doubt that you are working overtime from the ancestral plane, and if you have retained your stubbornness during your spiritual transition I have no doubt that you sit at a desk making sure what is for me shall never pass me by. This one is for us.

Thank you.